BEYOND HER
Reflection

Women Stories on Unmasking and
Standing Boldly in Their Truth

BEYOND HER
Reflection

Women Stories on Unmasking and
Standing Boldly in Their Truth

Tammy Woodard

BEYOND HER REFLECTION

Published by Purposely Created Publishing Group™

Copyright © 2018 Tammy Woodard

All rights reserved.

No part of this book may be reproduced, distributed or transmitted in any form by any means, graphic, electronic, or mechanical, including photocopy, recording, taping, or by any information storage or retrieval system, without permission in writing from the publisher, except in the case of reprints in the context of reviews, quotes, or references.

Printed in the United States of America

ISBN: 978-1-948400-41-1

Special discounts are available on bulk quantity purchases by book clubs, associations and special interest groups. For details email: sales@publishyourgift.com or call (888) 949-6228.

For information logon to: www.PublishYourGift.com

Dedication

This book is dedicated to God's greatest gifts: my sons Thomas Jr. and Damahje Bell, my mother Hattie Woodard (deceased) and my birth mother Vivian Shelton.

Thank you Momma Vivian for giving me life and loving me. Thank you Momma Hattie for teaching me everything about life and molding me into the woman that I am today. Although you are resting in heaven, you'll always be here with me. I love you both!

To my babies:

You two are the love of my life! I'm so thankful that God allowed me to experience unconditional love through you. Thank you for riding the waves of life with me even when you didn't understand. You are my earthly angels and I will forever love and cherish each moment that God allows me to spend with you! You are the wind beneath my wing. You have the favor of God over your life! You have greatness on the inside of you! Seek God to discover your purpose. Keep God first in everything that you do. You have the ability to do anything if you believe and trust in God. In time of doubt, recite my favorite Scripture: Jeremiah 29:11 "For I know the plans I have for you, declares the

Tammy Woodard

Lord, plans to prosper you and not to harm you, plans to give you hope and a future. Always remember that I LOVE YOU with all my heart!

Table of Contents

Acknowledgments i

Foreword – Cheryl Polote-Williamson xi

Introduction –Tammy Woodard 1

From the Depths of Despair to My Destiny
Eddie J. Bailey-Holden 5

Redeemed and Transformed
Lenase Shands 17

From Fear to Faith!
Michele Noel-Peake 31

Living the Bitter and Sweet
Felicia Evans Long 43

My Mother's Addiction
Juanita Payne 57

The Heart of a Single Mom
Sonya M. Hall-Brown 67

Married to Depression
Tonya Mackey Harris... 79

The Fight of My Life
Vatesha Bouler 93

About the Authors 105

Sources 115

Acknowledgments

All praises due to almighty God for without him, none of this would be possible. I cannot thank him enough for all that he has done and will do in the future.

I would like to first acknowledge Pulitzer Prize-nominated artist, poet, playwright, scholar, and publisher Mrs. Vivian Ayers-Allen for encouraging me to continue to write when I had a brief moment of doubt about moving forward with this project. I know now that God place you in my life for a reason. Thank you for pouring into me and sharing your knowledge and wisdom. I will forever be grateful for the love and kindness that you've shown me and my family.

I would also like to acknowledge my soror, mentor and Sister in Christ Cheryl Polote-Williamson for giving me the opportunity to tell my story and become a Best Selling Author for "Soul Talk" Book. Without you I would not be on this journey to change the lives of millions through writing and storytelling.

Most of all I would like to recognize my family, friends and all of you that have supported me along the way.

Thank you and may God bless you all!

Foreword

When we have painful experiences, we are often plagued with a myriad of emotions. Along with those complicated emotions, we usually have questions—lots and lots of questions. Questions like, *what did I do to deserve this? Why didn't this person love me? Why did this person hurt me? Why didn't God stop this from happening? Why me?* I know about these emotions and questions because I have had my fair share of them. Somewhere along the way (through my tears and pleadings with God) I heard Him say, *"why not you?"* You see, the thing about being in pain is that sometimes it can cause your vision to be blurry. When you can't see clearly, you cannot properly assess your situation. This was the case for me until I realized that I was asking the wrong questions.

God ministered to me in my darkest hour. He lifted my head and helped me to see His power in everything that I thought was going wrong. As He ministered to my brokenness, He restored my faith in Him and caused me to change my line of questioning. Instead of asking God 'why,' I started asking him '*how*' and '*what*?' I asked, *how can I make the best of this situation? What lesson do you want me to learn from this obstacle? How can I increase my faith in you?* When I started to ask the right type of questions, God began to answer me. His answers gave me the strength and determination that I needed to move forward. His word continually strengthened my faith. Although healing doesn't happen overnight, He has held my hand and kept my heart safe in Him through every heartbreak, disappointment and hardship. He helped me to understand that He chose me to endure the things that I was going through. He taught me to walk by faith and not by sight. His word tells us in Hebrews 11:6 (NLT), "And it is impossible to please God without faith. Anyone who wants to come to him must believe that God exists and that he rewards those who sincerely seek him."

Being chosen by God is not happenstance or something to be taken lightly. To be chosen or selected by God is a true honor. Of course, it doesn't usually feel good, but think about what it means to be chosen. He chose you because He knew that you would survive. He chose you because He knew you would overcome. He chose you because He knew that your heartbreak would be to your betterment, not your detriment. He chose you because He needed you to learn something. Most importantly, He chose you because He loves you! When we learn to accept God's choices, we can see His plan working in our lives.

The author of *Beyond Her Reflection*, Tammy Woodard, has allowed God to use her to transform the lives of others. She is a truly a woman after God's own heart. We have known each other over 25 years.

We graduated from the same college and are Sorority sisters of Alpha Kappa Alpha Sorority, Inc. After many years of friendship and sisterhood, she and I decided to collaborate on a book project with 19 other women titled "Soul Talk". Since then, she has become a Best Selling Author, which afforded her the opportunity for radio interviews and television appearances. Because of her integrity, leadership, and dedication, I have appointed her as Lead Ambassador of the Cheryl Brand Ambassador Program. Her mission is to help others discover their purpose while transforming lives through the power of storytelling. Through her vision for *Beyond Her Reflection*, eight women will unapologetically go beyond what the naked eyes can see, and reveal some of their darkest moments.

The eight powerful women in this book have learned to accept His choice. They, too, have made a choice. By sharing their testimonies, they have chosen to be silent no more. They have chosen to speak their truths. They have chosen to unmask their fears. They have chosen to be a voice for the voiceless. They have chosen to pour their hearts into these pages. They did it for you and countless others who have felt broken by life's various obstacles. They did it to bless, encourage and uplift you. They did it to remove the stain of shame that the enemy attempts to magnify. These women are true overcomers, and I know that their stories will minister to you in a way that will spark healing and change in your life. If you glean nothing else from the impactful stories of these women, I pray that you understand that faith and belief in God are the only things that will get you through trials and tribulations. May you always keep God's word at the forefront of your mind.

Cheryl Polote-Williamson
Multi-Bestselling Author
Award-Winning Philanthropist
Entrepreneur
Speaker

Introduction

Have you ever looked at yourself in the mirror? I know you might be saying, "Well that's a crazy question! Of course, I look at myself in the mirror every day." But have you really looked at yourself or are you looking at a reflection of you? What do you see? What do others see?

Most of us spend a great deal of our lives in the mirror focusing on beautifying the outward appearance. We make sure our hair, clothes, accessories (makeup and other things) are pleasing to the eye. We look to see if we've gained or lost weight. We use the mirror to prepare for speeches and even to take a selfie! What I'm really asking is, have you looked beyond the reflection and examined the man or woman in the mirror? Like you, for many years I glanced at myself in the mirror, focusing only on the outward appearance. It took a devastating event to occur before I stopped to take a long hard look, and I was not happy with what I saw. What I saw was a little girl who grew up feeling unloved because she was adopted. A woman who had held so much hurt and pain throughout her adult life.

A woman who had allowed herself to be overtaken by life's circumstances, so much that she didn't recognize herself. A 42-year-old divorced mother of two, bent but not broken. A woman that was good at masking the truth! For 30 plus years, I dedicated my life to taking care of everyone except myself. I had been a wife, mother, and a family/friend counselor for so long that I forgot who I was. I desperately needed to find myself.

One morning before I got in the shower, I stood in the bathroom, bare, looking in the mirror. I began to ask myself questions like: Who are you? Why did you allow yourself to go through the hurt and pain? How are you going to move forward now that you're divorced? I even questioned the way my body looked. But the most important question that I asked was, "God what purpose do you have for my life?" It was at that moment when "the mirror experience" came to be. The more I discovered my identity, the more I liked what I saw. God revealed to me that I needed to let the world know that there was more to me than what the eyes could see. I needed to reveal that there was more hidden behind the smile I always wore. He wanted me to share my story. Little did I know that I would co-author a book called *Soul Talk* with 19 other women. My "mirror experience" helped me discover my purpose and birthed the vision for *Beyond Her Reflection*.

In this anthology, you will hear from eight women who decided to unmask and stand boldly in their truth. You will see the obstacles that they had to face, and learn how they were able to overcome them. These women of God would like the world to know that they are no longer ashamed of their past, nor are they allowing minor setbacks to keep them from the promises of God. They want you to walk away seeing more than just your reflection. The purpose of this book is to serve as a guide to help you heal from the inside out. Also, to demonstrate that we have all been through trials and tribulations. Although we may have gone through the fire, we didn't come out smelling like smoke. My hope is that through these testimonies people will be transformed and share their story to release souls from bondage. I pray that you are blessed by the testimonies of these eight women. I pray that you, too, will look beyond your reflection in the mirror and discover what God has purposed for your life. Take that leap of faith and share your story with someone. Remember your story is not for you, it is to help others that are going through or have gone through. Your story has purpose, power, and the potential to change lives.

Enjoy and be blessed!
Tammy Woodard

From the Depths of Despair to My Destiny

Eddie J. Bailey-Holden

I pray that out of his glorious riches he may strengthen you with Power through his Spirit in your inner being.

Ephesians 3:16 (NIV)

On April 18, 1958, at Saint Agnus Hospital, on the campus of Saint Augustine's College in Raleigh, NC, I was born to Eddie Bailey, Jr. and Geraldine Newton Bailey. After having five daughters, my parents desired a baby boy, but to their surprise, I was delivered--another girl! So, I was named after daddy. Growing up with five older sisters, there was plenty of excitement in the household. I couldn't imagine being without them. The cooking, cleaning, babysitting, laundering, dishwashing, and the likes were their chores. In the meantime, my responsibility was to play baby sister and keep Mom and Dad abreast of their mischievous behavior.

My mother was a housewife by day and a Christian Evangelist by night. My father worked construction by day and chauffeured my mother to her services at night. She didn't have a driver's license. I don't know how he did it, but Daddy never once complained about taking Mama to her weekly revivals after working all day. Over a period of time, mama's life and Kingdom work heavily influenced his decision to accept Jesus Christ as his personal savior. In the Holy Scriptures, 1 Corinthians 7:14a (NKJV) reads, "For the unbelieving husband is sanctified by the wife, and the unbelieving wife is sanctified by the husband." They became partners in ministry. Their partnership worked this way in every part of life, even parenting. My mother was the disciplinarian, and my father was her enforcer. Together they raised us with high ethical and moral standards. Most importantly, they taught us to love the Lord and one another.

Mama accepted the call to the ministry when I was five months old, and because of her religious convictions, she reared her children in the church. We attended church so regularly that our extended family would question the time spent in these religious services. To my knowledge, my parents never responded, but they were following the doctrine of the Bible: "Train up a child in the way he should go, and when he is old he will not depart from it," Proverbs 22:6 (NKJV). Church and school were all we knew. The Christian way of life dictated our beliefs and actions. Although I was too young to remember when my mother founded her church in 1963, it introduced us to nothing but church, with no social life at all! I can recall being one of the first choir members and sitting in the last pew of the church, doing homework and falling asleep. I had very little social life. Growing up as a preacher's kid, it was expected that I would achieve a higher education. I knew that the only way to get from under their thumb was go away to college. That's what I called killing a bird with two stones.

During the fall, I left for college in another city about 45 minutes away from my hometown. Never having been away from home, I felt freer than I had ever been. I began to stray from my upbringing, becoming more engrossed in the social aspect of college than the academics. While attending parties and other social functions, I was first introduced to marijuana. Once I tried it, I liked it! In fact, I preferred smoking over attending class.

Mama observed the changes with me right away, but couldn't put her finger on the cause. She demanded that since I wanted to party rather than attend classes, I had to come home. "We don't have money to waste!" she said. I asked daddy if I could stay and he replied, "You heard yo mama!" I ended up quitting school and returning home. I didn't realize smoking marijuana was creating a habit, and the people around me were encouraging my usage. They were indulging themselves! Was I concerned? No. My friends were children of ministers, politicians, and educators. I was in prestigious company. Now that I look back on that period in my life, my motivation for smoking was very absurd. I must confess that I had an inferiority complex. Smoking with those friends made me feel important. I often ask myself why I felt that way. I wondered whether the feeling could have come from my spiritual upbringing. I refer to Proverbs 16:19 (NKJV), "Better it is to be of a humble spirit with the lowly, than to divide the spoil with the proud." I had convinced myself that feeling inferior was having humility.

Sometimes, while spaced out, I could hear a wee voice saying, "Your mama raised you better than this." I smoked more to drown it out. It has been documented that marijuana use leads to the desire for harder drugs. In my case, this proved accurate. My appetite for a greater high intensified. As a result of a broken heart from a former boyfriend, I needed a means to cope with the pain. I moped, sulked, and cried for days. There seemed to be no release from my heartache. I confided my troubles to my girlfriend, and she suggested something to make me feel better: cocaine. After going through the pros and cons in my mind, I concluded it couldn't hurt.

I was wrong. Every afternoon on my way home from work, I would stop by her house to indulge and talk about my broken heart. Eventually, we talked less about my troubles, indulging until my troubles were no longer the topic of conversation. She would share her cocaine with me; however, I felt the need to have my own. So my friend arranged for me to connect with her dealer. I was able to buy for myself. Our contact was always around and "holding," and I found myself buying enough cocaine just to take the edge of boredom off my ride home from work. After a few weeks, my use increased, until I was using every day. This went on for months. I worked harder to buy more drugs. Therefore, I did more drugs, so that I could work harder. This became a vicious cycle.

I always felt overweight, but using cocaine, I discovered I was losing weight. And I liked it! Family and friends asked what I was doing to lose weight. I would say, "Nothing." Mama recognized the drastic change in my personality and appearance, and warned, "Eddie Jean, what are you doing? You can get out here and get into something if you want to. I've taught you right from wrong, so you better use your head for more than a hat rack." I was transparent to my mother. Although things looked fine to others, my mama knew me. She knew something was wrong. She constantly questioned me about things and with my "Nothing" responses, she prayed openly around the house. She would kneel facing a chair while swaying back and forth, asking God to protect her children, to save them and right the wrongs in their lives; afterward, she would get up humming and singing a song to lighten her spirit.

Whereas the marijuana use was manageable, cocaine was addictive. At first, I went to work, but eventually, I would not go or make up excuses to leave early. I hung out with people who were more heavily involved in drugs than me, and I was fortunate to get out of some situations alive. Using cocaine gave me a "don't care" attitude. I thought of myself and what

I wanted. My father tried to appear unbothered by my situation, but sometimes he would fall asleep in a chair waiting for me to get home. I found him often saying, "You can get in trouble and get picked up by the police; I am not coming downtown for foolishness." In the back of my mind, I knew this was his way of telling me he loved me and that I needed to check myself. Still, I lost control and became addicted to the drug. I was far gone, but my faith in God began tugging at me.

My values changed. My family and I lived in the same town, and we were close-knit, but I didn't want to visit. I didn't have time for my old friends or even myself. I moved out of my parents' house so I wouldn't have to face them. I partied, went on buying (drug) trips, hung out all night long, all the while hearing my mother's voice in my head. As my addiction to cocaine intensified, my behavior grew more unpredictable. My close friends who were not involved in my lifestyle were no longer welcome in my world. I missed them dearly, but I just couldn't bring myself to communicate with them. I was ashamed of what I had become. My attention span shortened by the second, and I could not concentrate on anything. I wanted to stop using drugs, but they were too powerful to resist. I was shocked to be in the midst of influential people who were a part of the same drug culture from which I longed to remove myself. We partied, we got high, we shared stories of our lives, but most of all we shared that common drug that linked us together. Cocaine made us family.

By now, I was sleeping on the floor because I had sold my bedroom suit for $40.00 to buy the next hit. I had long since stopped eating, so my weight had dwindled by forty pounds. I couldn't keep money, had no food to eat, no drugs to share, and no car to drive. Then my roommate put me out of the apartment because I couldn't pay my rent. This sent me right back to the disciplinarian and the enforcer. Mama was glad to have me home. With me there, she could watch me, talk to me, and pray for me. But I felt trapped. I was overcome with guilt that they would witness what I had become. The embarrassment was unbearable knowing that my parents knew I had allowed myself to pursue this road of destruction. I had hit rock bottom. The drugs took control of my attitude, appearance, and most of all, my soul. I felt worthless. Without that personal relationship with Christ, I knew I was doomed. I had to do something. I realized it was time to confess my addiction to Christ and my family and ask for help. I wanted to salvage what was left of my life, no matter what.

The people I loved the most were the ones I had hurt the worst. But they were the people who took me back, like damaged property and supported my efforts of rehabilitation. Even though my family was there to help me and I wanted help, the urge to get high one more time was more powerful: jitters, anxiety, fidgeting, and insomnia. I knew I had to stop before something stopped me, but that aftertaste of cocaine on the back of my throat was lingering. When I was alone at home or riding along the highway, I would cry and scream, and ask the Lord to help me because I didn't want to live this way.

One Saturday evening about seven o'clock, I came across some friends I hadn't seen in a while. We began to talk, get high, drink and party. When the party was over, it was 9:30 a.m. I drove myself home, never knowing how I made it. Moving slowly, I managed to get myself out of my vehicle. I went into the house as my parents were dressing for church. Hoping they wouldn't see I was beyond intoxication, I slipped past them. My mother once told me that if I died, she would buy a black dress, walk behind my casket to the grave and cry, but come home and live. Those words always stuck with me, and that morning I wondered, "Is this it?" My heart was racing. I was sweating and having cold chills, but my body felt like an inferno. My lips were glued together, and all I wanted to do was lie down. Feeling as if I was overdosing, I struggled to maintain control of myself. An hour later, I knew it was useless. I panicked. I called to the church and asked for daddy. I think I asked for him because I needed his strength and sternness. I told him I felt I had overdosed and to please come home. I needed him. Not only did Daddy come, but he brought mama and four of my five sisters. My oldest sister took control. She stood me up in the shower, clothes and all. They didn't know what to do, but knew they had to do something. My other sister put on a pot of coffee. The other two talked to me while trying to hold me up and walk me. Then there was mama. Mama was praying like I had never heard her pray before. The entire house was involved in the rescue of my life. My sister called a well-known drug rehabilitation center and a counselor talked to me for more than an hour to calm me down. This situation was confirmation of the love that I knew my family always had for me. I thank God they were able to save my life! After hours of care, I was able to lie down and sleep. The next day, I awakened to find that my family was still there. They had not even returned to their homes and families that evening. I looked around like a new born baby and felt that this could be the first day of my life. I kept my appointment that afternoon with the counselor and began my healing.

My healing process began with a young man named Alex. He introduced himself to me as "Alex the Addict." My first thought was to ask for a female counselor. I didn't believe he could understand the origin of my addiction to cocaine. But as Alex began to speak, his voice became soothing and calming, which convinced me to trust him. He told me that everyone there was an addict and they all had different reasons for why they were there. He asked me, "Why are you here?"

At first, I wanted to say, "Because my sister called," but something else escaped my lips. I said, "I want help to rid myself of this terrible feeling." The conversation continued with questions and answers for nearly forty-five minutes. At the end of our conversation, Alex said I didn't talk like an addict, and maybe I just needed someone to listen. I knew God had already delivered me the night before. No doubt!

After I returned home, I talked with my parents and apologized for what I had put them through. My mother encouraged me to trust God for my complete healing. The test of courage and trust in the Lord began. For the first few days, unable to get drugs, it was hard. I was very irritable, physically weak, sweating with cold chills, had no appetite, and no desire to continue. My mother was right there encouraging me saying, "You can do it," and "let's pray." I prayed with all my heart. I yelled! I screamed! I cried! I prayed some more, asking God, why me? About seven days went by and I knew I wasn't out of the woods yet. Meanwhile, I called Alex. I called him many times until I felt guilty about doing it, but he never turned me away. The feeling of uncertainty and confusion continued for another couple of weeks. During that time, Alex became a friend, as well as, a counselor. Although I should have been a paying client, he extended his help after hours. He talked with me; cried with me; and spent long hours on the phone with me. For three weeks straight, Alex was there, until finally, I began to recognize myself. I noticed the sweats disappearing, the chills warming up, and my strength returning. It was a great feeling! In fact, this was the first time I had seen my mother smile in a while. My healing was in full bloom.

Months went by, and I was still clean. The slogan says, "Once an addict, always an addict," but my mind was made up and I wouldn't retreat. I had to hold onto my recovery, no matter what. I had been given a second chance and I seized the opportunity. The friends from the life that I had recently left behind were just that, left behind. I concentrated on what I could do to better my life. I still had my job and it became my priority. I enrolled in a local university. I earned my Bachelor's degree, which was my original plan.

I am not ashamed of my past, although it is not a life of which to be proud. My faith in God brought me up from the depths of despair to my destiny. I matriculated to Bible School, earning a Master degree in Christian Counseling and a Master degree in Arts in Ministry. I am now a licensed, ordained minister in my mother's church. If you ever find yourself addicted to any drug, I advise you to acknowledge it, pray, and find a support team that offers professional assistance. Rehab is not a quick fix.

BOLD REFLECTIONS

It takes one to commit to building a life where intoxicants are not needed to get you through each day. I am content with the path my life is on. I can testify from the Holy Scripture, "and we know that all things work together for good to those who love God, to those who are the called according to His purpose" Romans 8:28 (NKJV).

Redeemed and Transformed

Lenase Shands

1 I beseech you therefore, brethren, by the mercies of God, that you present your bodies a living sacrifice, holy, acceptable to God, which is your reasonable service. 2 And do not be conformed to this world, but be transformed by the renewing of your mind, that you may prove what is that good and acceptable and perfect will of God.

Romans 12:1-2 (NKJV)

BEFORE GOD'S INTERVENTION

I was mean and evil with the tendency to fight all the time. The hatred that I carried made me extremely rebellious towards everyone. But what I didn't realize, is that my behavior would lead me down the path of destruction.

I met the love of my life at the nightclub where I was working. He was very gentle and kind and showed a lot of affection, concern, and compassion for my family. He showed great compassion for my children.

There was nothing he would not do for them, and when people would ask if they were his children, he would say yes. I really didn't know what love was, but I convinced myself that this was it. For the most part, I was living in denial. The problem with being in denial is that you tend to ignore warning signs. Everyone around me could see them except me. By the time my vision became clear, and I started to pay attention, it was too late. I had allowed myself to become trapped in a toxic relationship. I was so in love that I never saw any wrong in what he did or the way he did it. In my eyes, he could do no wrong. Family and friends would tell me of his unorthodox behavior, but I never saw what they saw. All I saw was this beautiful man that I loved. I would see him with other women and ask about them, but he would steal my heart again, buying me candy, flowers, and other gifts. He would say, "You know I love you, you are the only one," and I believed it, never realizing it was all a lie because I loved him.

I was called so many bad names that it was normal for me to hear the words "bitch" and "dumb." Rarely was I called by my name. It didn't matter whether or not we were in public, the abuse did not stop. I would be so embarrassed to the point that I wished I was dead. I would be slapped, kicked or knocked down and stomped, while being yelled at and cursed. As time went on, the abuse continued, and with every incident, the intensity increased. I was thrown out of a moving car, hit with a baseball bat, and beat with a hanger. Still, I loved him. At the time, I thought he would change because, after all, he did love me, or so I thought.

I woke up one morning and said to myself, "I'm going to pack up and leave never to come back." I did this so many times until I just went numb. Whenever I did leave, he would come get me and convince me to come back home. I did this so often that he never took me seriously, so it was the same thing over and over again. This made everything worse, not better. After a while, it was back to the normal routine of abusiveness and wild behavior.

Back then there was no one for me to turn. Most people were taught to mind their own business and not get involved with domestic violence. There was no House of Ruth or shelter for battered women. To call the police was not an option either. I tried that once and ended up with ten stitches and a new threat. I often told myself that maybe if I showed him that I really loved and cared for him, the beatings would stop. I hoped that he would learn to love me the way that I loved him, but I was living in a fantasy world. In a month's time, he may have been good to me for a solid week. After that, it was back to the normal abusive behavior. It was so bad that he would change the odometer on the car to see how far I went and where I went. He wanted to know every detail of my whereabouts. He would take me to work and I could not be one minute late coming out.

It wasn't enough that he was abusive. He was also a cheater, and he paraded his women in front of me like it was nothing. He would pick me up from work, each time bringing a different woman with him. He never offered an explanation, and I was too afraid to question it. But in spite of his infidelity, he was extremely possessive. I spent many nights alone. I had a few friends that wanted just to come have coffee and talk, but they were afraid of him, so they would only stay for about an hour, then leave. Cell phones did not exist then, and I could not afford a house phone. The only way for me to make contact with anyone was to use the payphone on the corner.

When I did use the phone, most of the time, it was to check to see if anyone had heard from him. He would stay home all day doing nothing. Then, in the evening hours, he would shower, get dressed, and leave. He would tell me that he'd be back soon, and sometimes, it would be the next afternoon when he returned. The longest he stayed out was two days, and the clothes he wore when he left were not the clothes he wore when he returned. I believed him when he said that he stayed at his mother's house. Besides, I was told never to call anyone to check on his whereabouts, and whenever he discovered that I had, he became angry. He said, "If something happens, or if I'm in trouble, I will call you. So, to keep the peace, I became used to him leaving, and made myself comfortable with my children, doing things with them, and talking to anyone who would listen. But most of the time, I watched television and cried until I fell asleep. If I questioned him about where he had been, it was like he heard the sound of the bell in a boxing match. I could hear the announcer say, "Let's get ready to rumble," but of course it was a losing battle for me. Afterward, I would look in the mirror and become angry with myself. My eyes would have dark circles, and I would be missing a tooth, or have part of my hair torn out. I tried to never let my children see me crying or badly beaten. The one time they saw me cry, the only incident they witnessed, was when I was thrown out of the car. Otherwise, they heard the yelling and shouting matches, but they never witnessed the beatings until the day I decided to leave for good. I would make up some excuse like, "Mommy has a bad cold," or "I ran into the door."

I tried to confide in my mother, but she never believed any of my stories until she faced death herself. My mother was always telling me I should not be with this man, but like all young ladies, I did not listen. I felt I was grown, so she left me alone. But there came a time when I needed to talk to her. I needed her help, but she shut me out, so I stopped telling her anything. I always believed, she knew what was happening. She really loved her grandkids and would do anything for them. She would offer me to stay the night just so that the kids could stay also. I went along with that because I wanted my children to spend time with their grandmother. I felt comfortable because I knew my kids were safe. Through all the turmoil, I made sure my kids were not in danger. I was the only one in danger.

I will never forget that cold and windy day in Cleveland, Ohio. For some strange reason, this day felt different from all the others. I felt some sort of relief; I felt that I could handle anything that came my way. I was no longer afraid, and I was going to do what I needed to do, which was to go shopping for my kids. Usually on paydays, I did not spend any money until I saw him. This day was different. I did not feel the need to tell him or ask if it was ok to spend my earnings. I felt strong and confident. I was at my mother's house and decided to go to the store to purchase a coat for my son, who was in the 5th grade at the time. My boyfriend came to my mother's to get us. The evil that I had described to my mother reared its ugly head when he realized that I had gone shopping. He went crazy! He came to my mother's home looking for me. My mom insinuated that she knew about the abuse, and told him that she would not allow it in her home. She asked him to leave and that made him even madder. He pulled out his gun and pointed it at my mother's head, telling her to shut up. I knew I had to do something. I couldn't allow him to take my mother's life. I mustered up the strength and jumped in between them, begging and pleading him not to hurt my mother or my children. I told him that I would do anything if he spared their lives. Although I didn't know God at the time, he was watching over me. He let them live.

Scared out of my mind, I agreed to leave with him. It took a second—that seemed like forever—but he put the gun down. He then grabbed me by my hair, pulling me to the back of my mother's house. There were two sets of steps to the right, on the back of the house, with a total of 20 steps. He threw me down all 20 steps, dragged me by my hair, shoved me into the car, and continued to strike me like I was a punching bag. We drove around for a few hours; he knew that my mother was going to call the police and he would have to face the music. I cried my eyes shut. Then, he suddenly stopped the car and got out. As I sat waiting, I looked up at the sky. The moon was so bright. I don't ever remember seeing it that bright before. Gazing at that moonlight, I began to call on the Lord. I cried, "Lord, if I should die tonight, please take care of my mother and my children." After praying, I gathered enough strength to get out of the car, and I started walking. I had no idea where I was going, but I couldn't turn back. I guess God was waiting for me to decide that I'd had enough because little did I know, he stopped the car right around the corner from a Greyhound bus station. When I saw the station, I felt hopeful, and all I could think is that this was my time to escape. I was scared, and I didn't want him to find me, but I had to call my mother to ensure she was safe. After I spoke to my mom and confirmed that my family was okay, arrangements were made for me to leave on the next bus to Washington, DC. Still afraid that he would find me, I waited in the ladies restroom at the bus station for a friend to bring me a change of clothes and money. She purchased a one-way ticket for me and waited for the bus to depart. It was an 11-hour bus ride, but I never closed my eyes. I was too afraid to rest. I had never felt fear like that before and never wanted to experience it again.

AFTER GOD'S INTERVENTION: A NEW JOURNEY BEGINS

My aunt met me at the bus station in DC. She looked happy and relieved to see me. She said that my mom had called and told her everything. She told me not to worry because I would be safe there. Although those words were a relief to hear, I still felt unsafe. Even though I was hundreds of miles away, I was worried that he'd come after me. I kept having flashbacks of that night. After I settled in, I called my mom to let her know that I had made it safe. I think she regretted not listening to me all those time I reached out to her. I could hear it in her voice. My mother could not stop praying for me; she finally got a snippet of what I had been enduring. But she knew that God had other plans for me. After being in DC three months, I was finally able to find a job at George Washington University Hospital. Even though my life had taken a turn for the better, I was still afraid, angry and bitter. I did not trust anyone, so I built a shield of stone around me. It was the only way I felt safe. I was a loner with no friends, and I didn't trust any of my coworkers. My daily routine was work and back home to my Aunt's house. My uncle tried his best to get me to go out, but I refused to leave the house other than for work. After enduring 15 years of an abusive relationship, I hated men.

After a while, working in the George Washington University Hospital's Nursery Ward, I started to feel comfortable with my surroundings. My spirits began to lift. I started liking and trusting a few people.

However, I still had issues. I felt jealous of the ones who were, or seemed to be, in a good relationship. As I got to know some of the young ladies, it bothered me when I discovered that they were in an abusive relationship. All the anger that I had suppressed would rise and make my blood boil. It made me want to seek revenge for them. It seemed as though I was angrier than they were, but I had to remember that I was once in their shoes. God was showing me my past through the lives of these women. As I became more comfortable and trusting, I began to notice one particular nurse who was always happy. She smiled at everyone and never had a mean word to say. I admired the love she showed towards others. One day, my curiosity got the best of me, and I asked her, "How do you come to work every day so happy?" She looked at me and said, "Do you know the Lord and do you go to church?"

I laughed in her face and replied, "I don't need to go to church because they are all hypocrites! They are worse than I am!" Thank God she knew more than I knew and wasn't offended by my lack of knowledge. Instead, she invited me to her church. I don't know what made me accept her invitation, but I am glad I did. Attending that church service was the best experience of my life. While listening to the words of the Pastor, I became numb and confused. It seemed that every word he spoke was about my life. My first thought was that my friend had told the Pastor about me, and I was embarrassed. Before I knew it, I was crying so hard that a member in the church had to hold my child. One of the counselors came over, took me to the back, and shared the gift of salvation with me. At that moment, I confessed my sins, asked for forgiveness, and accepted Jesus Christ into my life. Since that day, my life was never the same. The chains had been broken. I have never felt better. I am now living. I now have hope, joy, laughter, patience, and peace. The chains that had me tied down have been loosed, and I no longer fear what man can do to me. I have been set free from sin. Romans 6:22 says, "But now being made free from sin, and become servants to God, you have your fruit unto holiness, and the end everlasting life." I was redeemed from all my sins, but I had much work to do. I started taking classes and going to bible study. I started working with several ministries in the church. I started wanting to help people instead of using and mistreating them. I opened up to trusting, loving and believing. The Bible says in 2 Corinthians 5:17 (NASB), "Therefore, if anyone is in Christ, he is a new creature, the old things passed away, behold new things have come." I feel as though this scripture was written just for me. God spoke to me through these words, and I became a new creation in Christ.

God has restored everything that the enemy took. I am blessed with a wonderful husband of 26 years, who has never hit or disrespected me. He loves me the way God said a man is to love a woman. I'm his helpmate, and he's the provider, protector, and priest of our home. Being submissive is a joy, being married to a wonderful man like him. I have three grown daughters to whom I taught that love is not shown by hurt or abusive behavior. I shared my story with them and encouraged them to be aware of the signs. I reiterated that I had been abused by a man in the worst kind of way, because I thought was in love, and believed he loved me. I warned them not to be charmed by good looks, smooth talk, and fancy clothes. They are tricks of the enemy, and once you are hooked and caught in the web, it's hard to get untangled. But if you trust and believe in God, he will deliver you from the snares of the enemy. You see, God made himself known to me. I never had a relationship with God, never knew of His powers, until I was placed in a situation where I had nowhere to run or hide. The only choice I had was to call on the name Jesus. God heard my cry that cold dark night in the car near the Greyhound bus station, and he delivered me from all that mess I was in. He kept my mother and children safe, and most importantly, He let me know that He loved me and was there for me all along. God wanted me to come running to him and not into the arms of my abuser. It is through his grace and mercy that I am here today. He had a purpose for my life and was not going to give up on me.

I am now a licensed minister, preaching the word of God to the unsaved. God already knew how things would turn out. I had no clue. Without God, I never would've made it. I thank God every day for saving my life. If it had not been for the Lord on my side, I would have died in March of 1975. I give God all the praise and glory. It feels good to live, love, and trust again.

BOLD REFLECTIONS

Affirmations: Speak Over Yourself

Women, know your self-worth. Abuse of any form is not acceptable. Learn to love yourself. You are fearfully and wonderfully made in the image of God. Life and death lie in the power of the tongue. So, affirm yourself daily by speaking life over yourself! Here are some affirmations to help you:

> *I am beautiful and deserving of all that God has for me.*
>
> *I am redeemed, bought with a price, for Jesus Christ laid down his life for me.*
>
> *I will no longer allow myself to feel ashamed for being a victim of someone else's destructive behaviors.*
>
> *I refuse to live in fear.*
>
> *I will love myself enough to seek help and walk away.*
>
> *I am restored, and I can now live out my days in peace without hiding, running, or being angry.*
>
> *I am a precious gift from God.*
>
> *God has a purpose for my life, and I will seek him to discover it!*

PRAYER OF SALVATION

Dear God in heaven, I come to you in the name of Jesus. I acknowledge to you that I am a sinner, and I am sorry for my sins, and the life that I have lived; I need your forgiveness.

I believe that your only begotten Son, Jesus Christ, shed His precious blood on the cross at Calvary, and died for my sins. I am now willing to turn from my sin.

You said in Your Holy Word, Romans 10:9, that if we confess the Lord our God, and believe in our hearts that God raised Jesus from the dead, we shall be saved.

Right now I confess Jesus as the Lord of my soul. With my heart, I believe that God raised Jesus from the dead. This very moment I accept Jesus Christ as my own personal Savior, and according to His Word, right now I am saved.

Thank you Jesus for your unlimited grace, which has saved me from my sins. I thank you Jesus that your grace never leads to license, but rather it always leads to repentance. Therefore Lord Jesus, transform my life so that I may bring glory and honor to you alone, and not to myself.

Thank you Jesus for dying for me and giving me eternal life. AMEN.

From Fear to Faith!

Michele Noel-Peake

Being confident of this very thing, that He who has begun a good work in you will complete it until the day of Jesus Christ.

Philippians 1:6

I will become who god says He created me to be.

How do you step out of the comfort zone of all you have ever known to embrace something that you do not know? How do you move from a place of fear to a place of faith?

My journey from fear to faith has been life changing. I could hear God saying back then that it was time for me to get out of the driver's seat of my life. Those weren't his exact words, but He began to speak to me in my circumstances and situations, through His Word. He was letting me know He was about to take me on a very different path than the predictable and expected path that I was on. It was like God was saying, "I know you have plans for your life Michele. I know you have 'things' that you are seeking in an attempt to have a good life for yourself and your family. But the plan I have for you is going to be much more fulfilling, rewarding, and lasting! I want to give you a life of impact over a life of things!"

I had to learn how to trust God to provide, and to guide me straight into His will and His way for my life. Previously, I had my own plans and idea's for my life and was in hot pursuit of them until He tapped me and said, "It's time to change directions, my precious daughter. I have something else planned, not just for you, but for your entire family."

It's not easy to move from a place of fear to a place of faith. But, when I finally did, it was not only life-altering, it was liberating and fulfilling.

TRUTH TRUMPS FEAR

I can recall several times in my life when I have felt fearful. Fearful to move forward and more so, fearful of a setback. And sometimes, the fear paralyzed me and kept me from moving at all. I knew deep down inside though, that I shouldn't feel this way. I believe God designed us this way because He says in His word that He has not given us a spirit of fear. I had a nagging feeling that I needed to change the way I was feeling, except early on, I didn't know how. My heart would race. In my mind were thoughts like, *"You can't do that!"* *"What are people going to think?"* But one of the most paralyzing thoughts was, *"What if I fail? What if it doesn't work?"*

Growing up in East Orange, New Jersey in a middle class family, I had one younger brother, and we lived a pretty normal life. My parents were loving and protective of my brother and me. One day after Sunday school, I remember walking away feeling fearful that if I didn't keep all ten of the commandments, God was going to be mad and punish me. This was a real fear, as I felt the need to "perform" for God, so that this powerful person I was learning about would love me. Back then, my Sunday school teacher did not do a very good job of sharing about God's Grace, or if she did, that was the Sunday I missed. So, for many years, I thought God only loved me if I was good. As a result, I put extra pressure on myself that I did not realize was there, and the performance spilled over into other areas of my life, like school. I had to get an A. I was upset with a B, and if I got a C, I thought the world was ending. I also did not want to upset my parents. This false belief that you have to perform at a certain level in order to be loved caused me to connect my value as a person to what I did and how well I did it. So I worked harder for the A just to feel better about myself. And this false belief spilled over into my young adult life.

FAITH FIGHTS THE STORMS

I was three years into my marriage to my high school sweetheart when we decided to start our family.

Children were a dream of mine. I tried to eat right, exercise, and even stop the occasional drink on holidays, because I knew we wanted to have a child soon. But devastation hit my life unlike I had ever experienced. There was a problem. Our struggle was not in getting pregnant. It was holding the pregnancy, and I had very early miscarriages. We were ecstatic each time the pregnancy test showed up positive, and devastated with each loss. I never thought in a million years we would struggle to have children.

After the third miscarriage, I could hardly take it anymore, and I began to question God, asking, "Is this you punishing me for having a previous abortion?" I could not figure out what I was doing wrong. Then doubt and fear set in. I had the fear of not being able to have children. I began doubting God's love, His forgiveness, and His grace and mercy. I was still struggling with the mindset that performance was the only way God would bless me. It created the perfect opportunity for me to exercise my faith and trust God at His word! Hebrews 11:6 (ESV) says "And without faith it is impossible to please him, for whoever would draw near to God must believe that he exists and that he rewards those who seek him."

After three very long and difficult years of losing babies, I was able to carry a child. I will never forget what it felt like when I finally made it to the second trimester. There was this feeling deep inside me that made me feel this one was it. Although nothing changed in me physically, I held on to what I felt was a promise from God, that I would one day have children. And nine months after that fourth pregnancy, God finally answered our prayers and blessed us with a baby girl!

As faith would have it, two years later, God blessed us again with another daughter. My faith had grown. I began to realize that God's timing is everything. Not only did I fall in love with these precious gifts from God, my daughters, but I found myself falling more and more in love with this man that I had never seen personally, but who seemed to have my back in ways I could not have even imagined. And it was powerful.

FAITH TRUSTS THE STILL SMALL VOICE

I remember taking off a couple of days from work for some much-needed rest, and on the last day, decided to paint an accent wall in my bedroom, which was very therapeutic. As I painted away, my mind was quiet. My husband was at work. The girls were in school. There were no racing, stressful, or negative thoughts running through my mind. I was in a calm place mentally and emotionally. I was listening to my favorite Gospel station when all of a sudden, I heard a still small voice inside me say, *"Michele, hand in your resignation."* Prior to this divine moment, I wanted to leave my job of 18 years to be home to raise my children, who were five and seven at the time. I wanted to start my own business and find that thing that God had really called me to do. But, I was afraid. I was afraid to leave without first knowing I would be okay, that "my stuff" would also be ok. I was afraid to leave without feeling completely and utterly secure that I had everything covered first. Notice I said that "I" had everything covered. That meant having little to no bills, cars paid for, etc. I even remember saying the year before that I couldn't leave unless I got a financial package from my job.

Looking back, that wasn't faith at all. Wanting and needing external security is not wrong, but when God is saying "I have you," and we ignore Him, that is a problem. My faith was in what I could see and what I could touch. The numbers had to add up; the money had to be right, and the feeling of comfortability had to be there. After all, that's how I was raised. It just seemed like good, plain-old common sense. So I was scared—part of me was anyway. There was a desire inside me that felt way more powerful than I could put into words at that time. It's like I had forgotten that God had brought me through pregnancy losses and still blessed us with children.

After hearing that still and small voice, I replied back with a gentle, "Ok God." It was as if someone was in the room with me, talking to me, and convincing me that everything was going to be ok. It is hard to describe the peace that came over me from that surrender. That day, while painting my accent wall, listening to gospel music, and thinking about God and His peace, I found it. I felt so light, no longer burdened by the constant barrage of thoughts of "what if," that were plaguing me. What if he (my husband) can't handle everything for our household? What if we lose everything we worked so hard to get? These questions were put to rest.

I made up in my mind that I would hand in my resignation when I went back to work that Monday. I had finally said yes to God, and no to all of my doubts and fears. I arrived at work on Monday and sat down at my desk, determined to move on what God said. And before I could even get my day started, my phone rang. It was my supervisor on the other end, sharing with me that the company was offering—go figure—a financial package for management employees who wanted to take advantage of a buyout. He asked if I would be interested. I could have just fainted right there on the phone. I said yes to God on Friday, and He said yes to me on Monday morning!

FAITH BRINGS CONFIRMATION

Before receiving the call from my boss that Monday, I had had a conversation with my husband about leaving, and he said "I think you should," and wrote me a letter saying, in so many words, "It's time for me to take care of my family." My husband supporting my decision to leave was the 1st confirmation of what I heard from God. The call from my supervisor was the 2nd confirmation. Needless to say, I said yes to the package!

My third confirmation came two weeks before I was due to leave, and it was when a woman ran a red light and hit me head-on with my daughters in the car. I was knocked slightly unconscious until I heard my youngest say "Ouch!" I rushed out the car and jumped in the backseat to find that both of my girls were okay. My youngest had even taken off her seatbelt. It could have only been by the Grace of God that she was not thrown into the front seat of the car.

For a moment, I thought to myself, "I had a reliable car with no car payment, and now I have to get a new car." I could feel myself getting ready to think, "I can't leave now." But I heard that still small voice again say— as I was looking at my reliable transportation riding away on the tow truck— *"Michele, yes. Yes, you will lose some "things" on this journey. But, what matters most, I will keep for you."* Mathew 6:33 (NIV) says, "But seek first his kingdom and his righteousness, and all these things will be given to you as well." I turned around and looked at my two little girls sitting on the curb next to the police officer, unharmed by this major accident. At that very moment, in my heart, I said once again, "Yes God." I knew instinctively, that He meant He would keep my family intact, that whatever fear I had of losing things could no longer control me. I had to focus on him, and him only! The question was not whether or not I should leave. The question for me to answer was, do I still trust God? At this point, I was beginning to understand that the ultimate act of faith is truly obeying God, in spite of how you feel, and in spite of what you think.

FAITH GROWS

I realized God was using every struggle in my life up to this point, to build my faith and trust in Him! Every level He takes us to is going to require another level of faith and trust. Walking in purpose requires faith, trust, and guidance.

The day I came home with my first daughter after having those three miscarriages, she stopped eating and became very lethargic. After several hours of trying to keep her awake to eat, as instructed by the hospital, we noticed she started to turn gray. So we took her back to the same hospital that had discharged her that morning, to end up having a medical evacuation to the neo-natal intensive care unit at the children's hospital for the next five weeks of her life. Doctors told us they didn't know if she would live or die. It was at this time that my faith grew by leaps and bounds. I had to once again trust God and put her life in His hands. In spite of feeling the fear of losing her, Faith prevailed!

I guess the decision to leave my job on faith, wasn't as hard as it could have been once I focused on what mattered most to God! And when I look back and see that if God bought us through that life or death situation with our first-born daughter, why was I so worried about whether or not to leave my job, to be home with the child that God saved and blessed me with? When I compared the two, it was no contest. God saved our baby. God brought me into this world, kept me protected and safe, and brought me out of every single trial.

FAITH OPENS THE DOOR TO PURPOSE

I can't say that the decision to leave my job made common sense in my mind. I could never clearly explain to people, as bad as I wanted to, what was next on my agenda. It felt awkward for me not to have an answer, but I didn't. I thought about saying many things, but the truth was, I simply did not know. All I really knew for sure was that I heard God and decided to trust Him.

It was not until I began to spend more time with God, talking and listening to Him through prayer, and reading His word that He began to reveal to me I was already walking in my purpose. He told me, "I am just going to expand and enlarge your territory." I remember the day He told me to preach His Word. I got up that morning and decided I was going to have lunch with God, and get in His face so I could hear Him clearly about my next steps. Who would believe I would leave the beach that day with God revealing that I should preach His Word?

God is always there, just waiting for us to acknowledge Him. We were created to worship Him, to diligently seek Him, and to do what He needs us to do, when He needs us to do it. We will never know what He has in store for us, if we don't believe Him, trust Him, hear Him, and obey Him. If I look back over my life's journey up to this point, I have to say that I wouldn't change a single thing. I wouldn't change all the times I felt fearful. I wouldn't change the painful moments or the times of great loss. It was those moments that brought me closer to the creator of all of Heaven and Earth. He opened my eyes to the woman He intended me to be. He made me stronger in my walk with Him. And most of all, He is no longer this powerful invisible force I learned about in Sunday school, who punishes you if you don't keep the Ten Commandments. Today, I call God my friend. HE is someone I trust in the dark places to provide the light. He is someone I rely on daily for strength, guidance, wisdom, direction and to simply breathe. I'm eternally grateful that He chose me to go from fear to faith and with Him, you can too!

BOLD REFLECTIONS

Here are some tips for personal reflection:

- Accepting Christ is the prerequisite to a transformed life full of faith, hope, joy and power.

- Once you accept Him into your life, you have to believe that He is who He says He is, and trust that He can do what He says He can do in His Word.

- Then, when you hear Him call your name, in that still, small voice, don't ignore Him; answer Him.

- No matter what He is calling you to do, accept, surrender, change, walk away from or forgive, always tell God yes!

Living the Bitter and Sweet

Felicia Evans Long

For I am now ready to be offered, and the time of my departure is at hand. I have fought a good fight, I have finished my course, I have kept the faith.

2 Timothy 4:6-7

It was a January day at the Inner Harbor in Baltimore, Maryland in the late nineties. This particular weekend, I had initially decided to veg out and stay home. But, my friends talked me into having dinner at the Inner Harbor. When we arrived, I had no idea that a few gentlemen would be joining us. As we came to our table, there were two empty seats side-by-side. I sat in one and Tim sat in the other. Our conversation started because he couldn't decide what to order from the dinner menu. So, I offered a few suggestions. Our conversation spilled into the evening while walking along the Harbor. We talked about the south versus north, our families, fishing, and many other things.

He was a funny guy with a contagious laugh. At the end of the night, we exchanged phone numbers. He walked me to the car before making the drive back to Newark, New Jersey, and I went back to Silver Spring, Maryland. That night, he nicknamed me his "southern belle." He liked the idea of me being from North Carolina. Years prior, I relocated to the Maryland area with the support of my Uncle Gary. He always said, "I want you to see the world." A few years after college, I decided to take my uncle up on his offer and relocate to Maryland to work on my master's degree. When I arrived, I was a little shocked by the cost of living, having to take the metro to work, and all the traffic. Because it took me some time to adjust to the area, I delayed starting graduate school. My uncle was very instrumental in introducing me to city life and helping me to make the transition from southern to city living.

COURTSHIP

Six months later I received a telephone call. When I answered, the voice on the other end said, "How are you, it's Tim." Unable to place him, I asked, "Tim who?" He replied, "Tim from the Inner Harbor." He said, "I misplaced your number and just found it," and "I would love to see you again. How about a fishing date to Ocean City, Maryland?"

"Sure," I replied, thinking to myself, "How can I be cute on my first date in fishing gear?"

We set the date and he arrived in Maryland about two weeks later with a fishing vest and red fishing rod for me. He scheduled an eight-hour fishing trip, but I wasn't sure if I had eight hours' worth of conversation for this first date. As fate would have it, we missed the eight-hour boat and took the four-hour fishing boat instead. It was truly the best first date I had ever experienced. When we made it back to shore, Tim ordered us frozen drinks and we talked on the pier and watched the water.

By 2000, we were officially dating. He was building his career at NYU Hospital for Joint Diseases in New York, and I was working in Maryland. We traded the travel time—he would travel to Maryland and I to Newark, New Jersey. This went on for five years. Then, in early February 2005, he asked me to be his wife. I said "Yes," in love with the platinum princess-cut ring he presented. I felt so much joy and knew he was the partner for me. With his gentleness and authentic, unconditional love, I knew I could love him forever.

NEW BEGINNINGS

In September 2006, we married in Raleigh, North Carolina, surrounded by our loved ones, and spent ten days honeymooning in Costa Rica. We later settled down in Rockville, Maryland, and Tim began a new career at George Washington University (GWU) Hospital in Washington, DC. He adjusted well to our new life in Maryland, immediately gaining professional friends, and was favored among many of the surgeons at GWU Hospital. As a southern wife, I enjoyed getting up in the morning to pack his breakfast and lunch. His colleagues called him "spoiled." While at GWU, he traveled and participated in mission assignments to Guatemala and Guyana. He enjoyed his profession and making a difference in the healthcare industry. When he traveled to these mission assignments, it was always hard to see him leave because I would miss him so much. But I always looked forward to his safe arrival home. I enjoyed being a wife and catering to my husband. My days were always filled with tasks from preparing dinner, picking up laundry from the dry cleaners, or grabbing a movie from Blockbuster and later, Redbox.

While I was in graduate school in 2008, life got busy for us, but we still made time for each other. Between our regular routine of working, it was typical for us to do things together, especially going to the movies and baking. Tim enjoyed helping me in the kitchen, from chopping up vegetables, to just being good company while he watched me cook. He provided my life with adventure. In 2011, we marked our fifth wedding anniversary with a surprise trip to London, Paris and Scotland..

After finishing graduate school and earning a Master's of Business Administration, and taking a break from a doctoral program, I told Tim I would like to open a small business. I always had a love for confectionery, my favorite being gumballs. In 2012, we decided to open up an old-fashion candy store in my hometown of Lumberton, North Carolina, called Sweet Candy Café. We secured the storefront and recruited friends to help us clean and prepare for the store's grand opening that November. We were about 28 days from opening up our first store when we received a call that it was on fire. I was devastated and had to be comforted by my brother while Tim was in route from Maryland via Amtrak. Many thoughts ran through my mind, including the fact that we didn't have renters insurance. We were going to get renters insurance but felt we didn't need it until we were officially open to the public. We had no additional financial resources to pour into the store, so I called all our vendors and explained what happened. I showed them a copy of the newspaper because I was on the front page, carrying from the burned building a few things that I was able to salvage. There were not many usable items after the fire. Most of our acrylic candy bins melted, and the candy was destroyed from the water and smoke. Even the unopened candy was no good. Although we were nearly derailed by the fire, Tim talked me into rebuilding. Most of our vendors were kind and replaced inventory that we had purchased.

Thankfully, the building landlord leased us a new building. With help from the Lumberton community and our friends, we opened in November 2012. We were excited to be business owners. Because of Tim's work schedule, I traveled to North Carolina often, and he went with me when his schedule allowed. In November 2013, we celebrated the first anniversary of Sweet Candy Café. Our flagship storefront was progressing well and the community welcomed our small business. While promoting Sweet Candy Cafe, sadly we learned my uncle had passed. This brought tremendous sadness to our family. He had a long-term career with the government, was an amazing old-school swing/hand dancer, and had always been the life of the party. He was also the reason I relocated to Maryland. I was concerned about my mom because she was extremely close to her baby brother.

THE BREWING OF COFFEE AND A SILENT STORM

Late one evening in April 2014, we received a call that my older brother was in an automobile accident in North Carolina and was air lifted by helicopter to a specialty hospital. My mother was in route to the hospital and I was in a panic in Maryland. Tim held me in his arms tightly and continued to tell me, "Your brother will be okay." Before receiving the call from my mother, I was sitting on the floor with my husband, crying while he said a prayer. I was very impatient because I wanted so badly to know what was going on, but Tim encouraged me to wait until my mother called. I was wondering how bad the accident was because my brother had to be airlifted to a local trauma hospital. When mom called, her voice was so weak. She said, "Felicia, I did all I could do by asking the doctors to do whatever it takes to save this life, but he was gone." Because my brother's accident was so severe, he was thrown out of the truck he was driving, and the truck landed on his body. Hearing my mother share those details, I fell apart thinking about the pain my brother had suffered. I was broken as his baby sister, and I couldn't imagine what grief my mother was feeling because that was her first-born, and only son.

Losing my uncle in 2013, then my brother so soon after, I was very worried about my mom, especially because she lived alone. As a southern mom, she's really tough. She lost her mother when she was only a teenager, so she had learned to deal with pain privately. I worried about mom not because of the things she said, but because of her silence. She didn't talk about it or mention it. I would often bring up loving memories about my brother to my mom over dinner or while we were out shopping. We reflected on the good memories we shared and not the tragedy of losing him. When I wasn't around, I asked friends and family to make special visits to check on my mom to ensure she was doing okay.

To keep my mother busy and active, I asked her to help with planning the details of Tim's 40th birthday. He would often ask me what it felt like to be 40, since I was older. I would always respond with a sweet smile and kiss on his lips. So, at the beginning of the year I started to plan for his 40th birthday extravaganza in Nevada. He knew about Las Vegas but didn't know that I had invited many of his childhood friends and colleagues to join us. I secured the venue in Las Vegas and mailed out the "Save the Date" notices. I wanted it to be a birthday to remember. That summer, Tim insisted that I attend a family reunion in upstate New York. For some reason, this particular reunion, he insisted that I take a break from the store to attend, and I did. It was another great road trip. It was wonderful seeing and meeting family members that I had never met. Tim and I even managed to beat a few family members over a game of spades. He loved playing cards, from spades to poker. More importantly, it was just great to be with my husband, surrounded by my extended family.

In July 2014, Tim told me he was traveling with his childhood friend to Los Angeles in August. We spent so much time together that I thought it was a good idea for him to have a weekend trip with his friends. It was important to me that he had a lot of fun leading up to his birthday weekend in Las Vegas the following month. August 14, 2014 arrived, and it was the night before Tim's departure to California. Like many times before, I helped him pack his clothes, including his blue swim trunks. We had a conversation about the trunks because I thought they were too big, but he convinced me that with the drawstring, he would be fine. He reminded me that the flight was early and if I wanted to, he would call a cab because he hated that I would have to get up so early. I assured him that I didn't mind and he said, "I'll make it up to you when I get back."

He was on an early flight out of Dulles International Airport (IAD), so we were up before dawn. Tim grinded some coffee beans for a fresh brew, got dressed and waited patiently for me to get dressed, while sipping his coffee. This morning felt extra special. There was a nice breeze in the air. We arrived at the airport much sooner than we expected, so we sat in the car, talked and laughed, and watched yellow cabs pull in and out the airport while enjoying our coffee. When he got out of the car, I got out too. He kissed me passionately and said, "I can't wait to get back home to you," then planted a final kiss on my forehead. I watched him walk through the glass doors of the airport.

As I drove to the office that morning, he sent me a text and photo to let me know he made it on time to his flight. That weekend, I was not traveling to Sweet Candy Café, so I spent the time running errands and ordering candy for the store. I spoke with Tim later that Friday and he had arrived safely in California. That Saturday, while he was in Los Angeles, we talked and I told him I had a long day, that I was going to bed early, and told him how much I loved and missed him. I told him to have a good time and he said, "Okay." Shortly after, he texted me confirming his return flight information to Maryland, and my response was, "Super sweet." He responded, "You're the best wife ever. I can always count on you."

On Sunday, August 17, 2014, I took a pot roast out of the freezer to cook. I wanted to surprise Tim with his favorite dinner when he arrived home. I texted him that morning, "Please confirm your flight is on time baby." Shortly after that, I received a call. The voice on the other end of the phone said, "Mrs. Long?" I replied "Yes. I'm sorry, who is this?"

"Is this Mrs. Long?" he repeated. I said yes.

He was a doctor with a Los Angeles hospital. "Mrs. Long, he said, "early this morning, your husband was rushed to the hospital because he was unresponsive."

I was silent, and so was the California doctor. Then he spoke again, saying, "Mrs. Long, I'm sorry. We did all we could, but he drowned. We tried our best to save him."

I cried and pleaded, saying "Please. He's all I've got. Please save his life." But he repeated everything again, saying "I'm very sorry for your loss." From that point, I don't remember saying very much. Grief still takes over every time I think about that moment. The last thing I heard the doctor say is that Chaplin at the hospital would be calling me. It felt like my heart had stopped beating, like a piece of me was being ripped from my soul. I just could not process that I would have to live the rest of my life here on earth without him. Months prior to his death, I had gone to see a specialty doctor because we had decided to start a family. But we would never have the opportunity to be parents.

I pulled myself together just enough to phone Tim's parents. Nothing made sense, and I'm not sure if I even believed what was happening. It was a silent storm that I never saw coming, losing my uncle, my brother, and then my husband. I went from planning his 40th birthday to planning his funeral.

We have always had the support of family, friends, sorority sisters and Tim's colleagues, but it was essential during his funeral, and in the many months that followed. Tim's colleagues chartered buses to travel to North Carolina from Washington, DC, to provide me and our family with love and support.

For the first few months, my home was filled with many people stopping by, calls, police wellness checks, and mailed cards of kindness. But before long, everything stopped, and the reality set in that my husband was not coming home. Trying to cope, I slept in his undershirt because I could smell his body in it. When I didn't have it on, I held it up to my face. This may seem morbid to others, but for me it was therapeutic.

Some days I feel withdrawn from the world. While still heavily in this grieving process, I have found that some people pull away from me socially because they don't understand my level of grief. I don't think less of them; some just don't understand. From grocery shopping, to sitting at the table for dinner, it's a routine reminder that things will never be quite the same in my life.

PROCESSING THE PAIN OF GRIEF

Living with grief takes a lot of emotional energy. There are times when I cry all day. I isolate, and feel extremely lonely. I miss the life that I shared with my husband. His absence is constant in my mind. I miss his touch, our intimacy, and all the ways he made me feel phenomenal. He was my partner in everything for 15 years. Laying my sweet husband to rest was one of the toughest things I have ever had to do. It is a harsh reality that everything we discussed for our future will no longer be.

From this life experience, I would say that everyday actions, like sending your loved one to the grocery store or taking them to the airport, are anything but "routine." They are indeed a gift, not to be taken for granted, given how suddenly life can change. Releasing the pain and anger of losing my life partner will make room for me to heal. My method of coping has been to stay busy. I have also joined a grievance group with certified counselors. I routinely visit Tim's grave during my visits to North Carolina. There have been lots of prayers, and I speak of him in the present tense. It is life changing.

My life's mission changed. Although Tim and I were not parents, we loved children. In 2015, I founded the Timothy Rodney Long Memorial Scholarship Fund. Every August 17, I award a scholarship in my husband's name to a student at a Catholic Preparatory School in Newark, New Jersey, where Tim graduated in 1992. I have also founded Tim's Toys, a community event where we donate Christmas toys to two families in Newark, NJ or Lumberton, NC. Every December in my husband's healthcare memory, we donate items to pediatric patients who are in the hospital during the holidays.

In January 2017, Sweet Candy Café started and introduced its first cohort of Candy Kids Wear Blazers, a program that teaches young girls about entrepreneurship and hospitality. On November 25, 2017, Sweet

Candy Café's fifth store anniversary was dedicated to Tim, and a portion of the proceeds were dedicated to his namesake scholarship. Tim was a good soul with a contagious laugh and zest for life; he balanced me. I have accepted what God allowed, but it doesn't stop the hurt. I miss my husband. I miss my friend. I push past the pain by getting up, getting dressed, and focusing on what I can do to make a difference, the kind a legacy I want to leave for the next generation, and the select community service projects that, through me, will reflect the life that my husband led. When people see me, I want them to see Tim.

I strive to stay centered by focusing on his life and not his death. Some may call my grieving process courage, but it's important to me to make my husband proud in the long journey ahead. I will forever remember his love, and that final kiss on my forehead. I hold on to and cherish, the fond memories that we shared. He was a fantastic mate, and he was perfect for me. I pray often, and I ask for guidance. I hold fast to my faith and know that I am not walking this journey alone.

BOLD REFLECTIONS

If you have gone through a similar situation, here are a few steps to help you move forward and overcome:

1. Mentally decide that you will not look how you feel.

2. Find a prayer or words of love, and whisper them softly to yourself.

3. Understand that others will not fully comprehend your pain and grief.

4. There's no time limit for grieving. Be sure to take all the time you need; it's your process and no one else's. Understanding that you may lose some friends and kinships along the way but it is okay. Caring friends and family, who love you unconditionally and without expectations, will understand and be there on the days when you can feel the sunshine and the wind on your face, and on the days when you can't.

My Mother's Addiction

Juanita Payne

But they that wait upon the Lord shall renew their strength; they shall mount up with wings as eagles; they shall run, and not be weary; and they shall walk, and not faint.

Isaiah 40:31

GOD'S EMBRACE

Smart. Intelligent. Loving. No nonsense. Go-getter. Hard worker. Kind. Caring. God-fearing. These are just a few words that describe my mother. I still remember the shrill cries and terror piercing through my body the day my sister said, "Juanita, she's gone." The feeling that came over me is unexplainable. The entire house was silenced as I cried from the pit of my stomach. My children ran to see if I was ok, and my nephew put his arms around me as if God himself had come from heaven and embraced me. I never envisioned my own mother passing away. She was my strength and my rock. My heart broke as my sister described how they cried out, as the paramedics made continuous attempts to usher life back into her limp body. She was frail and unresponsive, and by the time she arrived at the hospital, she had passed away. I'm thankful to God that my mother and I had an awesome relationship. I called her almost every day. Margaret Payne, my powerful matriarch succumbed to a massive heart attack, after 52 years of smoking and drinking. One important thing she told me was, "Juanita don't worry about me. If anything ever happens to me, I know how to call on the Lord." Those words were like poetry; they resonated within my soul. Prayer was all I had. But in my time of pain, I knew it was God alone who kept me.

SURVIVAL – HUMBLE BEGINNINGS

"When you pass through the waters, I will be with you; and when you pass through the rivers, they will not sweep over you. When you walk through the fire, you will not be burned; the flames will not set you ablaze."

Isaiah 43:2 (NIV)

Growing up, we did not have much. My mother made due with what she had. After graduating from Elkhorn High School in West Virginia, she moved to New York, where she met and married my father several years later. To make ends meet, she saved almost seven thousand pennies for the down payment to purchase a new home for her growing family. Lavish furniture and decorations were costly, so she was only able to afford a pair of wingback chairs that sat in opposite corners of the living room. My siblings and I never realized how poor we were, but looking back, I see how God kept my family. My mother was a survivor and was never afraid of hard work. Her mother had been hard-working, and her father worked in the coal mines of West Virginia, so my mom had great role models in her early life. My mother's strength and survival techniques came from seeing her own mother's faith in God and closely watching her mother care for herself and nine other siblings. There was no such thing as staying away from church on Sundays; my grandmother knew that God was her ultimate source. They had a garden and kept animals. They slaughtered their own pigs and ate everything on the pig, from the snout to the feet. Resourcefulness and a commitment to finding a better way of life were skills that my mother inherited from birth. She kept those virtues alive throughout her life, and she instilled them in me.

I often wondered how two parents could afford to care for ten children on a modest income. In my mother's era, there was no such thing as running to fast food restaurants. Instead, my grandmother believed in home cooking. One of her favorite recipes was for made-from-scratch glazed donuts and cinnamon buns. It was like eating Krispy Kreme donuts from heaven! The taste of those donuts brings back many memories of West Virginia and my early childhood. Those were some of my happy memories, but they are joined with other unhappy memories, like the times when my mother and father fought.

FRIGHTENED BUT COVERED

Above all, love each other deeply, because love covers over a multitude of sins.

I Peter 4:8

One afternoon, while my siblings and I were at home, we heard rumbling noises, like thunder, coming from downstairs. We made our way down, one by one, and stacked near the door like dominos to watch. My mother screamed, "Get out! Get Out! Don't ever come back!" She raged, kicking my father between the legs. The table lamp that sat by the front door was in pieces, and a few fragments contained blood from my father's head. We watched as he stumbled out of the front door to never return. As my siblings and I grew older, we learned that our father had stolen our mother's welfare check to feed his drug addiction. That was the first and only check stolen, and it led to divorce and the breakup of our family. Throughout that ordeal, my mother never expressed any underlying fear. She continued to stand on the promises of God through prayer. All she could do is seek the Lord and his strength.

Even after my mother and father divorced, we had fond memories of Christmas and appreciated all of the sacrifices she made for us. It was always a joy when Christmas came. My mother placed candles in the windows of our house, carolers would sing in our front yard, and we made it a tradition to play in the snow. One year, my mother managed to get four popular dolls home for Christmas. She worked for a toy store, and with the little money she made, purchased each doll one by one. There was no such thing as a bad Christmas. My mother did her absolute best to give her children the best lives possible. Despite being so poor, we never missed a meal. Knowing how she pressed on despite insufficient pay, and lack of support from an addicted husband, I understand why my mother would always say, "Lord, be a father to my children." She prayed as she cooked, and gave thanks before we sat down to eat, as if our lives were a living Proverb, as if Jesus himself came down and fed us, along with the five thousand. She knew how to stretch meals, not so much in the natural, but with her prayers. Providing for her daughters was always at the forefront of her mind, despite being gripped by her own vices. But those vices soon put our lives in jeopardy.

MY MOTHER'S ADDICTION

God is our refuge and strength, an ever-present help in trouble.

Psalms 46:1

My mother passed out from drinking and left a pot on the stove. "Juanita! Get up, or you are going to die in this house," my sister yelled at the top of her lungs. I was only five years old at the time, and could not fathom or process death. To this day, I remember how loud one of my sisters screamed. I didn't know what to do, but my sisters quickly grabbed flour and emptied the entire bag over the burning pot on the stove. I thank God that they were able to put that fire out—and the two that came after. The cause for each of them was the same. My mother passed out after drinking, with a pot on the stove. As more fires happened, we realized that life would force us to react under pressure, and more importantly, we were responsible for saving ourselves. These fires were like monsters in the closet, ready to consume anything, to cloak our furniture in layers of dark soot, and to fill every crevice of the house in a billow of smoke. I remember sitting on the porch steps, wiping the soot out of my nostrils while waiting for the smoke to dissipate. Dealing with an alcoholic parent was not easy. But God had his hand on us. We could have lost our lives. But he covered us. There was no damage to anything in the house.

I was in denial of my mother's addiction, until the day she came to my fourth-grade recital, drunk. I was overjoyed after I played my recorder. The applaud we received was breathtaking. When we went back to our seats to wait for the recital to end, I noticed that two of my classmates were laughing, saying look at that lady over there. "Where?" I asked. They pointed to a lady two rows over to our left. When I looked, to my surprise, it was my mother. I sunk down in my chair with shame, embarrassment, and fear that someone would know it was my mother. I wondered how she made it to my school. When I left that day, she was in no condition to come. She had been drinking all day. I left the recital in a hurry and later found out that some of the neighbors recognized my mother and escorted her home. She was struggling with her demons and alcohol was her escape.

My mother told us stories about living in haunted houses as a child, and about some of the perils she faced while in West Virginia, all of which led to her addiction. My older brother came to live with us when he was 18. Born during my mother's time in West Virginia, he lived with my grandmother, helping around the house until he completed grade school. After he graduated, it was my mother's decision for him to come live with us in New York, to help with my siblings and me. A few years after he moved in, there was another fire. I remember hearing my brother yell, "Move! Move!" The kitchen curtains were ablaze. Before being grabbed and taken outside, I had been staring directly into the fire. I couldn't believe we were facing the same thing again. I knew God was there, but I was angry, scared, and hurt.

Despite some of the things that my siblings and I endured, we learned to handle my mother's addiction with love. I learned to laugh a lot, and found solace in playing fun games with my sisters. We would act like we were camping, making tents out of blankets in the living room. We would even take turns sliding down the stairs on a blanket, each taking a turn, while one was at the end of the staircase pulling the other one down. As I got older, my mother's behaviors did not change, and I still needed an escape route. Laughter was my escape. When I met my husband, he provided that for me. We would go to the movies, comedy shows, and dinner. Spending time with him allowed me to forget.

MARRIAGE

So they are no longer two, but one flesh. Therefore what God has joined together, let no one separate.

Hebrews 19:6

I met my husband in a department store in New York. The connection we had was wonderful, and we enjoyed each other's company. After many dates, laughter, and conversations, we fell in love and decided to get married. "Juanita," my mother said, "I want you to go further than I did in marriage, and make sure you feed your husband." She was married for eight years, and that was the only advice she gave me. I remember telling her, "You don't have to worry about me; I'm never getting married and I'm staying home with you." To my surprise, I was the second of my mother's children to get married.

We were wed on October 22, 1989, and during our marriage, had three amazing children. Listening to my mother's advice, I desired to stay married through the ups and downs, and allowed God to be my compass. I never knew how strong I was until I had been married for 22 years. Who would have believed that so long a marriage, to a person that brought happiness to life, would later end in divorce? He had no desire to work on the marriage and left the family. Raising our three beautiful children was both rewarding and challenging. As a single mom, I put my children before myself. I wanted to make sure all of their needs were met. Financially, it was difficult. Where there were two paychecks before, after the divorce, there was only one. I still had to work, cook, and clean, but the children were helpful too. I found my strength as a single parent because I watched my mother take care of my siblings and me. Her faith in God and her prayers allowed her to care for us. I found myself doing the same thing. Above all of my pain and heartache of watching what my mother went through, I now know that God kept her, and he kept me too. There were times when I did not have enough money to feed my children, but God allowed me to make a way out of no way. Having faith and maintaining a strong belief in God is what has gotten me to this point in my life. Through it all God kept me.

BOLD REFLECTIONS

And the peace of God, which passeth all understanding, shall keep your hearts and minds through Christ Jesus.

Philippians 4:7

Remember that despite the trials and tribulations you are going through now, God will keep you. All we have to do is pray, believe, and have faith in God. There will be times when you tell people what you've endured, and they do not fully understand. But God said he will not leave us or forsake us. In our darkest hours, we need to get on our knees and pray to God for guidance.

The power of prayer is a mighty weapon that we can use at all times. Don't be afraid to call on Him. He is just a prayer away! God has designed our lives to be victorious, and he gives us victory over the tyranny of our circumstances and the problems we encounter.

And let us not be weary in well doing: for in due season we shall reap, if we faint not.

Galatians 6:9

Time to refocus! Let no one or nothing interfere with your destiny. You are destined for purpose. Your life has been set apart. Can you feel the pull in your heart to be better, to go beyond? Stop looking at what is tangible. Go back to the beginning, and remember that you walk by faith and not by sight. Faith will allow you see the unseen. It is time to refocus. Pray always, and worry about nothing! In times of trouble pray to God get on your knees ask God to give you peace.

The Heart of a Single Mom

Sonya M. Hall-Brown

But they that wait upon the LORD shall renew their strength; they shall mount up with wings as eagles; they shall run, and not be weary; and they shall walk, and not faint.

Isaiah 40:31 KJV

My mother said that on the day I was born, the 11th day of February, it was like a day of paradise in Bronx, NY." I grew and developed such confidence and assurance because I had both parents sharing their love with me. They both were providers for their one and only baby girl. As I grew, I treasured so many moments: going on vacation, having my own bedroom and toys, feeling my dad's protection. I didn't have to share my love with anyone else; I was daddy's little girl, and I made both my mom and dad proud of my academic achievements. Nothing in this world was able to distract me—until I turned 14.

My world turned upside down. My parents grew apart. They were getting a divorce, and I had to choose with whom I wanted to reside. That was the most difficult, heart-breaking, darkest experience I'd ever faced. I was asked to make an adult decision with a child's mind. My father's actions towards me and my mother, made me feel as if his love for me was fading away, but my mom's heart was always radiant towards me. She was my friend and confidant. But I was angry with her and my dad. Although my dad would repeatedly say I was still "daddy's little girl," life changed, and I didn't feel like daddy's little girl anymore. I felt lonely and abandoned. Later, my father seemed as if he had forgotten about that unconditional love he once shared with me. Months passed without having any form of communication with him, and it left me feeling more deserted. I was given opportunities to spend time with my dad's side of the family, but little time with him.

I sat in the hallway of a courthouse, scared, trembling, and trying to hold back my tears while my parents were with the judge. I was bitter and angry, thinking to myself, "My dad has left me. What did I do to deserve this?" I thought that I was the reason for my parents' separation. I didn't consider how my mom must have been feeling.

I was called to the judge's chambers where I was asked which parent I wished to live with. My response shocked the judge when I said, "Neither!" I was so angry! I said to the judge, "I want to go live with my aunt in New York." I was not thinking about my mother's broken heart. I wanted to go somewhere I thought was better than where I was. The judge shared my response with both of my parents, and they agreed to allow me to go for one year to live in NY with my aunt. They thought that maybe the grass was greener on the other side. I would be given a better education. But it was a life-changing experience. My mind and heart were engulfed with anger and bitterness towards both of my parents. I didn't realize how fearful, lonely, and vulnerable I was. I was only 14 when I went to New York. I had to learn how to share my space with others, something I wasn't accustomed to doing. Sharing my space to sleep, taking turns being on the floor with a padded mattress or in a bed. Having to ask permission to eat something verses eating anything I wanted at any time. My wardrobe was very limited. I wore the same clothes over and over, although my mom could design and sew anything I wanted to wear. There were times when I set aside my pride and borrowed from my cousins' closet, but this was a true-life adjustment. I had to develop better social skills in order to have friends at school. If my cousin didn't get along with someone, they were not my friend either.

My idea of socializing, was going out on the terrace when I was bored, to look down and watch the activities across the street at the corner store. One day an attractive guy was standing on the street corner watching and smiling at me each time I engaged in his view. He inquired about me to my cousin, and later, I was given the opportunity to meet him. He made me smile, then my smile turned into laughter. Somehow, he knew how to make me feel better about myself when I wasn't feeling my best. We became friends, though he was much older than me. He lavished me with good food and gifts. He treated me like I was a porcelain doll, with the kind of care that I used to get from my dad. His presence replaced my loneliness and the void my father left. I began to cut school and share valuable time with him. I enjoyed having him around, and it became a relationship. I didn't know much about the birds and the bees yet, and I had unprotected sex with him, not understanding the risk of diseases and pregnancy, which was my first mistake. My mom only gave instructions not to engage in such activity, but we never had detailed conversations about the consequences of having unprotected, premarital sex.

According to court orders, the time came for me to return to South Carolina with my mom. During my return, I was so ill that my mom and aunt had to seek medical care for me. I found out then, at the age of 16, that I was pregnant, and the father was miles away in New York. I was like a deer in headlights, confused and afraid. But I refused to make contact with him about our baby (mistake number #2), not understanding that it was the right thing to do whether he accepted the child or not. So, I became a single mother.

I continued with my schooling until the day I gave birth. My daughter was born on my 17th birthday, and what a birthday present she was! The love I felt for my black pearl was indescribable. I felt the rhythm of her heartbeat and how it synced with mine. In that moment, I made a promise to her and to myself, that she would never want for anything, especially love from her mother. Philippians 4:19 says, "And my God shall supply all my needs according to his riches in glory by Christ Jesus." And he did supply.

I began the journey of motherhood holding my sweet baby girl, keeping her clean, well-dressed, fed and warm. The birth of my daughter gave meaning and purpose to my life. This time, *she* filled the void and healed the pain of the relationship with my parents. I never wanted my daughter to feel abandoned or alone, because that was the way I once felt and something I know other teenage mothers suffer from. After bonding with my daughter for six weeks, I returned to school, and my mom and I worked together to raise her. My mother taught me how to be responsible for my actions, so I knew it was my responsibility to provide for my daughter. I got a job at a local business, and worked every day after school while my mom babysat. I'm grateful to say my mother was never forced to purchase milk, pampers, diapers, or clothing. She only contributed on special occasions like holidays and birthdays. My job and supplemental government assistance supplied my baby's needs.

After graduating from high school, I applied to several colleges, and was accepted to each one. I chose to attend Shaw University in Raleigh, NC. My mother and I agreed that she would keep my daughter while I furthered my education, but she reminded me, "I will help you with this child, but with the next child, you're on your own." I had almost completed the first semester of school when I became ill again. I was sick morning, noon and night, and only felt better when I slept. I had met another young man that I had fun with, and I was pregnant again! I asked the Lord, "What am I going to do with another baby at 18?" I was so afraid to tell my mother. Initially, I avoided telling her because I wasn't ready to embrace my fears. Instead, I took a different approach. I had enough money saved to cover up my sins, thinking that an abortion would be the easy way out, and that my mother would never have to know. This time, like the last, my plan did not include the father. I asked myself, "Have I not learned from my first mistake?" But my mind was made up, and I thought my decision was clear, so I made arrangements to proceed with an abortion. I used the yellow pages and made contact with a prochoice clinic. When I arrived, my hands were trembling while signing in. In pre-op, I saw films of the procedure, and it wasn't a pretty sight. I waited for my name to be called, and knowing this was not the right thing to do, I began to cry uncontrollably, and rushed to the ladies room.

Seeing me in distress, a lady at the clinic held me in her arms and said, "You are not forced to do anything, so relax and listen to your heart." I must have been cognitively impaired, but a spiritual warfare was happening. My heart was pounding during the preparation for the procedure. The spirit of God, along with my upbringing and my conscience, would not allow me to go through with it. I shocked the medical staff, and myself, when I shouted, "Stop!" I took the lady's advice and listened to my heart. My heart would not allow me to kill this innocent baby in my womb, who was depending on me to make decisions for it to live. The procedure was cancelled.

Later, I found the courage to return home. I purchased a bus ticket with the money I was going to use to abort my child, to come home to my mom and face my fears. I left my school books, clothes and other small possessions, and went to the one I knew would never turn her back on me. It took all the strength I had to announce to my mom that she was going to be a grandmother for a second time. I expected a beat-down sermon, and I waited for her to tell me how much stress I had contributed to our family. But she said not a mumbling word. I was shocked at her silence. Her response concerned me greatly because I wasn't sure whether the news was causing her mental or physical harm, or if she just wasn't surprised. But I remembered her telling me that with a second child, I was on my own. Her silence sent me into survival mode, forcing me to think quickly. I once heard a preacher say, "The teacher doesn't talk when the test is being given, he only monitors." I figured this was the test.

The timing was perfect for me to make provisions for my babies. I was expecting a tax return that would cover my expenses for a while. My mother knew I could survive this storm. I believe her faith in God, and in me, was beyond measure. She allowed me to execute that strength and faith through her silence. God's Word says, "I can do all things through Christ who strengthens me" Philippians 4:13. I believed and trusted God at His word.

God may not come when you want him, or the way we would like him to come, but He's always on time. I found a nice, cozy apartment that was fairly new and that accommodated my income. I was able to pay all the necessary deposits and the rent for six months in advance. I had great credit, which allowed me to purchase inexpensive furniture for my new home. It felt good to share with my mom my great accomplishment of providing a safe place for my girls. However, her concerns about not having my daughters near her caused her to break her silence. My new place was over 35 miles away. Addressing this, she said, "But you don't have a car. What are you going to do without a car? Who will be able to keep the kids while you're working, and how will you be able to get to and from work?" I didn't have a clue, but I knew that God had always encamped his angels around me, and everything would be alright. I knew He would supply all my needs, and by faith He had never failed me. I failed him, but He never failed me. My mom just shook her head. She was worried. But I had watched her as a single mom. She taught me how to cook and how to clean. She showed me how to give respect to my father even though he abandoned me. I watched and learned from her and my godmother, how to survive with the bare minimum. I knew I would make it.

When I said God will supply your every need, it is because I know it to be true. My aunt gave me a van to drive until I was able to purchase my own car. My uncle, cousins and friends would always give me money for gas to travel. I met a beautician who did my children's hair and my hair. She became very close to me and seldom charged me for her services. She never charged for my children. Her home was always open, as if I was her daughter. I became so close to her and her family that she and her husband were godparents to me and my children. Many people offered hospitality without grumbling. As I look back over my life, I was a rebellious young lady after my parents divorced, but God was so merciful and gracious. God still blessed me with good paying jobs to provide for my children. I am an ambitious lady, and I never give up on my dreams. My goal is to leave a positive impact on my children and children's children, and to be wholesome and independent, putting God first in everything I do. My mom, and others who had an impact on my life, taught me to always believe in the power of prayer.

My life choices led me to become a single mother for many years. I chose not to include the fathers in my girls' lives. I understood later that that was a big mistake. I learned that we can't make decisions for God, assuming one thing or another, but that we must give God room to work. I was selfish and angry. But I should have told the fathers of my children that they had daughters, whether they accepted them or not. It is God's job to work on a mother or father's heart and conscience, to do what is right for the sake of their children. When my girls were preteens, they had the opportunity to meet their fathers. Friends and family members were eager to introduce my girls to their fathers, without my consent. But I had to muscle through my pain and give my girls what was rightfully owed to them, and it wasn't as bad as I thought it would be. It was God's divine plan that by the time those meetings occurred, the girls' fathers and I were mature enough to co-parent in a way that patterned the word of God. As it is written in Hebrews 12:1, "Therefore, since we are surrounded by such a great cloud of witnesses, let us lay aside every weight and the sin which cling so closely, and let us run with endurance the race that is set before us." My daughters are now mature young moms who are implementing the strength, truth, and ambition that was instilled in me by my mother, and that I instilled in them. My mother transitioned to be with the Lord in January of 2013, but once a mother, always a mother, and her legacy lives on.

God has blessed me with a husband, whom I love dearly. My husband graciously accepted me as I was, flaws and all, and he accepted my girls as his own. He has been our priest, our protector, and our provider. He has been a caring husband, a loving dad and outstanding grandfather for our family. We have been blessed with three daughters, two sons, and three grandchildren.

Jeremiah 29:11-12 say, "For I know the plans I have for you, declares the Lord, plans for welfare and not for evil, to give you a future and a hope. Then you will call upon me and come and pray to me, and I will hear you." With those words, I encourage all single moms and dads to challenge yourselves and reach towards your goals. Rest assured that you and your generation will achieve greatness. Everything is birthed in the mind. There is no such thing as "I Can't!" You must see the vision before it can materialize in the natural, but first you must look for meaning in your life. Surround yourself with positive people. Understand that, regardless of your circumstances, you have to have goals and a plan to get from where you are, to where you want to be. Live your dream! Be humble and always put God first. You will achieve more than you ever thought possible. Your children are depending on you so that they may live.

BOLD REFLECTIONS

As I look back over my life, I know that this was the journey that was predestined for me by God, even in my trials and tribulations as a single parent. If I had to re-live my life, I would not change a thing. My father and I still have an estranged relationship, but I know he loves me, and I love him. I no longer dwell on what was and how life should have been. I am grateful and profoundly changed because of my daughters.

I have forgiven myself for having children out of wedlock, and God has forgiven me. I have forgiven myself for stressing and worrying about what people think. I have more than I could ever need. I am deeply loved and profoundly blessed because of my daughters.

Married to Depression
Knowing the Signs

Tonya Mackey Harris

I can do all things through Christ which strengtheneth me.
Philippians 4:13

WHAT WAS I THINKING?

How could a smart, young, professional, church-going woman, not have the ability to pray for the right man? When you have a plan that doesn't align with the plans that God has for you, there are always lessons to learn. I lived through this very powerful lesson for almost 20 years. On paper, he looked exactly like what I envisioned. You know, the one you put on your vision board. I built in my mind that a smart, quiet, strong man, with a manly voice, was a template for happiness. When I met him, he had not stepped out into the world yet and was somewhat green. He had so much potential. And did I tell you he was fine? Too often, that alone is enough to block a smart woman from looking deeper into a man.

Mr. D did not appear on the scene right away. That spirit grew into my marriage as we both focused on our careers and treated each other like a second or third priority. It made it easy for our union to crash and for depression to find a new home. I sometimes wonder if I was choosing to live with my "eyes wide shut," because I had a vision of us being an amazing Kingdom power couple, the type of couple you see in your church, that appears to be doing Kingdom things, are role models to their children, and who always looks happy. You assume that they pray together, and that everything is going their way. I thought to myself what amazing kids we would have. I even thought, "I bet he would make beautiful babies." I focused on the idea of how great our lives would be together. I was in my early 20's then.

It was a good relationship for most of the first year. He was what I thought he would be, and was always so caring about my welfare. That man could look at you like he was listening to the best words ever spoken. He made me feel so valued and understood. I found this most appealing. We did all the things that normal folks do, going to work, coming home on Fridays to have hot wings or fried fish, coleslaw and French fries, and going to church on Sunday. But, everything has a season, and our seasons changed faster and faster every year.

MR. D'S FIRST VISIT – SHOW AND TELL SIGNS

The first time I met Mr. D, he was somewhat mysterious. He would come to Georgia, where I lived, and later to the Midwest, to visit. We had a ball in those early days. Those days were like any other new relationship—good! Then one day he started to show me another side, a side I don't even think even his family knew. That side would sleep for hours, have limited conversations, and later, disappearing acts. I remember coming home from work one summer day when he had apparently started to prepare some chicken. He had let the chicken sit on the kitchen counter the whole day, until I came home. When I walked in the door, the house smelled horrible. He said that he just could not get up the energy to finish what he started. I thought it was odd, but did not think any more of it.

Shortly after, things took another turn. He had landed his first job in his career field, and we were excited. But shortly after he started the job, I received a call from them, saying, "Mrs. Harris, we are looking for your husband. Is he home? He hasn't reported to work in two days." I did not know what to tell them. I thought he was at work. I wondered if I should lie and make up a story to help him keep the job, or whether or not I should call the police. I did not know what to do. So I cried. I called his mom, and she did not know what to do either. I prayed, and I cried. I could not believe this was happening.

It was like being married to a ghost, someone that you could not catch or find if you tried. The depression symptoms grew from excessive sleeping to very limited conversations, to secretive behavior. Mr. D consistently disappeared with no form of communication at all. It was a lonely time for me. As his wife, I did not want to tell anyone of my concerns. My feelings ranged from not wanting others to know there was something wrong with my great husband, to not wanting to be identified as a failure in my marriage. I did not want anyone to know that I did not have a grasp on what was really happening. Besides, I was the strong one. I felt betrayed and abandoned, because this man, to whom I was so loyal, was not just struggling with depression, but was also having an affair. I wondered if I was the problem. Was I too sarcastic? Did I not cook enough? I thought it might be that he was so conservative. Did he mean to marry a white lady instead of a pecan tan? I was conservative, but still a "sista" around my family and friends. I represented the strong black woman and was not as gentle since I was hurt in the past. I thought that maybe I was too strong for his taste. It felt as if I could not break through to the man I thought I married. What was worst is that his pattern had no specific formula.

WHEN DOES X + Y = DEPRESSION?

The sum of the equation, $x + y = $ depression, took me 15 years to solve. The formula kept changing. One day, $x + y$ would equal us starting a partnership with a business associate that could take us to the next level financially. At other times, $x + y$ equaled him managing million-dollar contracts and growing in his company, then suddenly disappearing from work, home, and life for weeks. Then there were times, x + y equaled affairs (in-person or virtual).

Because I was no mathematician, I kept a journal. In this journal, I would have prayers, specific scriptures, dates, timeframes, missing-person's reports and a resolution section. This last section of the journal helped me keep track of the details when it was time to file a report with the police. I remember being so embarrassed at having to call them, and having them at our front door, as neighbors looked on. When you think you are a part of a power couple, you don't want neighbors and family to see or know what is really going on inside of your home when it is broken.

For me, x + y equaled sadness. Over the years, the depression episodes grew stronger and stronger, laced with affairs. The two seemed to always equal to more disappearances, which were a byproduct of guilt I'm sure he was dealing with. I would have family come and go, raising the question, "Where's Mr. D?" I would always act as if I did not hear the question, while holding back the tears.

On one particular occasion, my beloved grandmother made a surprise visit to us from North Carolina. We stood in the kitchen, later joined by my mom and dad, the kids and their cousins. With so many people around, I was operating in production mode. Then came the question, "Where's Mr. D?" As always, I acted as if I had not heard them, and started cleaning. I must have washed and rewashed every dish in the house that day. But the follow-up came.

"Did he have to go into work today?"

I took a breath and said, "He is gone."

My grandmother asked, "Gone where?" Answering this question for my family was one of toughest things I ever had to do. I told them that he struggled with depression and that sometimes it became so overwhelming that he just disappeared. At times, the disappearances were due to his sex addiction. His doctors called his sex addiction a trigger, an event or situation that causes a person to become depressed from their actions. I told them about Mr. D's diagnosis of bipolar disorder. I explained that I was told to think of it as if he were wounded internally, and no one could see him bleeding inside. When he had a bipolar episode, it meant he would have days, both good and bad, that could lead to depression for him. I told them that sometimes, if it was bad enough, it led to suicidal thoughts.

The silence was loud in those moments after I spoke. It was as if I had told them someone died. They simply could not believe it. Then came the look, the look that comes when people who love you, feel sorry for you. For my grandmother, the look was accompanied by sadness. She had lived a similar life before me, with an alcoholic. From my mother and father, the look was of total heartbreak. But then I said to them the words that kept me strong in every one of those trying moments of my marriage, "This too shall pass."

I recall saying to them, what I know to be true. "God will never leave me or forsake me, even in the midnight hours." He was there when I was alone, crying silently in the bedroom so the kids would not hear me. That day in my kitchen was the day I learned about the true love of family in a time of need. I had tried to keep them from finding out what was happening in my home, because I did not want to be a failure to my family, yet they showered me with love once they knew. We ended that day hugging each other, loving on one another and singing songs of praise, while eating some soul food.

A KEY TURNING POINT

The moments of rest were great. It seemed after he returned and put us back in a state of normalcy, that we might have a chance to bounce back. I felt comfortable enough to take a new job; we even spoke with his job to make sure his position was secure despite the disappearances. Then, I took my first business trip to Philadelphia. On my way back, I received a call, the kind that you can't respond to right away, you just listen. It was the kids' daycare. The voice on the other end of the phone said, "Hi, Mrs. Harris. This is daycare center manager, and I'm calling because it's 6 pm, and no one has come to pick up the kids." I replied, "I'm sure their dad is just running a little behind. Let me give him a call."

I called, and the cell phone immediately went to voicemail. That moment was one of complete helplessness. In my world, it was the call of death because voicemail represented a message from Mr. D that said, "I have checked out. Can't tell you when I'll return." I sat there on my flight, my face and hands numb, and my legs feeling lifeless. I could not believe we were here again, going backward, and feeling each time as if the spirit of death was visiting me. Then God showed up. I received a call from a sister in the church, who was just checking on me. I put on my production voice and greeted her with love. Her response was, "Your voice sounds sad. Are you okay?"

I said, "I'm on an airplane right now, heading back home, but I just received a call from the daycare saying that Mr. D has not picked up the kids. I don't know anyone that I can call that isn't on their pick-up list." I felt so extremely vulnerable sharing this with a sister, an Elder in my church. I felt overwhelmed, and I hated him for putting me in that situation. I felt like once again I had given my trust to a man who could not be there for me, and I allowed him to betray me in a way that impacted our children. I started to cry and felt that at that moment, I had to totally surrender to whatever God had next, and let it happen. Don't get me wrong; it wasn't quite a freeing feeling. But it was a feeling of knowing that I had done all I could. I felt as if I had no other choice but to allow someone to help me, by God's grace. The sister from the church said, "Honey, you call that daycare and tell them their grandmother is coming to pick them up, and I'll be there in 30 minutes. I got those babies. You just get home safely, and you can pick them up from my house.

"Write down my address," she said, "and don't worry because you know that God's got you!" I started to cry again and just sat there in tears with a gentleman on my right and left, that did not say a word to me. Their silence told me they heard my conversation, but they did not speak.

There was a moment on that flight when everything was completely quiet. The plane's engine and the sound of air flowing were all could be heard. In the stillness of that moment, I thought about what the sister from the church said, God has me—and I fell asleep. When I finally landed and traveled to the sister's house to get the kids, I thought about what could happen differently this time when he returned. I decided to do some research. This time I would encourage him to see a better doctor, to try out different meds, and maybe go into a facility for a little while to take care of himself. The kids and I would go and see someone as well. It was a turning point for me. I understood mental illness much better, but I also learned why I chose a Mr. D in my life. Through the wives support group, I had an opportunity to look at myself. I went into therapy and discovered that I was drawn to rejection, betrayal, and abandonment because I saw examples of that in my childhood. Initially, this realization felt overwhelming. I recall going home and falling into a depressed state. I started to think about how Tonya the child felt, and how that child had hoped for greater days as an adult. But as an adult, I was feeding into the same behaviors that I fought to get away from. I began to understand my attachment to Mr. D. In many ways, his rejection felt like home. I learned of some tools that helped me balance being a caregiver, and relearned how to love me in the process. After going through this process, it all started to make more sense. I was able to understand how his choices aligned with his illness. When he did return, he agreed to a new doctor and different meds, but we could not afford for him to go into a mental health facility. He promised he would take his medication this time, and seemed to be committed to doing the work. He was really doing well. A year passed, and there were no signs of depression or bipolar disorder. Life felt like it was back on track.

THE NUMBER 8 MEANS NEW BEGINNINGS!

The saying goes, "If things are going too good, get ready for battle." That is exactly what happened. The kids were at summer camp, and it was going to be a great parent's home week. Since we were work-a-holics, we agreed to only work late on Monday, and that we would spend the week working to rebuild our relationship using the tools we learned in marriage counseling classes at church. I got excited about just going to the movies and spending time at home alone. The evening came, and I sat there waiting with dinner cooked, candles lit, a little wine, and no husband. After waiting several hours, I called the office to learn from the janitor, that no one was ever in the building after 6 pm. I called him on his cell, and although he answered, his voice and tone were different. He talked to me like he was speaking to his little girl. He clearly had someone with him in the car. He did not return home that night. The next day, I got a call at my office from a lady I did not know. She asked, "Are you Tonya Harris?" I told her that I was. She responded, "You may not know me, but I have been dating Mr. D for six months. At the time, I was having a strategy meeting in my office with our CEO. I politely asked her if I could call her back. I left the meeting with my boss and ran to my car to give her a call back. When she answered, she began to tell me how her friends Googled me, and that I looked just like her.

She was number 8, the eighth of his sex addiction triggers. She represented for me, a moment where I could choose how I wanted to handle this situation. Number 8 meant a new beginning. I was taught that the number 8, biblically, means new beginnings. I believed this to be true for me because I felt a release the moment I had a conversation with her. I told her that I chose not to be an angry woman and explained my intentions. Number 8 gave me an opportunity to reassess what I wanted next in my life. So, I chose divorce. I chose to start life over with just me and my children. But I also had one more task. I had to apologize to Mr. D. I had to apologize to him for hating him in my heart. I know you are thinking, why in the world would you apologize to him? It's simple really. I had to apologize to him for the unspoken hate, and all of the contempt I had towards him, from the years of affairs to the moment he missed picking up the children, to number 8. I never said it, but I knew the hate was there in my heart all those years and I had to put an end to it. So I prayed before he came over to pick up his clothes, and I apologized. He looked at me like I was crazy. But I knew in my heart that this moment was one that would be pleasing to God. I wasn't concerned with his actions. I wanted to walk away from this relationship giving him genuine forgiveness. The moment I asked him for forgiveness, as hard as it was, God immediately began to bless me for my obedience. I knew I had to say it with genuine love and respect. It had to be the Christ in me because at that moment, I had no other intention but to be pleasing to God.

No matter who or what your Mr. D is—bipolar disorder, mental abuse, bad boys, enabled men, whatever it is—with God there is forgiveness. He can move even the highest mountains on our behalf. I am a living witness. I have lived through divorce, breast cancer and symptoms of mental illness in my son. But through it all, I refuse not to give God the glory! If I had not been married to Mr. D, I would not have my two children, whom I adore.

God is an ever-present source of help in the time of need. These moments presented for me a testimony that I have been privileged to share with you well after it has passed. And you know what? It did pass! It is gone. My equation finally equals peace and unprecedented favor. It is as if God put me into a pressure cooker, and once I was done, He gave me rest. Rest for the moment, then rest from the enemy preventing me from successfully thriving.

BOLD REFLECTIONS

There are three things I would like to reader to walk away with after reading my story:

- Build awareness of the potential signs of mental illness experiences in your mate.

- Consider the potential impact on any children you may have.

- Know that with God's grace, prayer and faith can change things and give you the strength to make it through the storm (Philippians 4:13).

The Fight of My Life

Vatesha Bouler

Heal me, O LORD, and I shall be healed; save me, and I shall be saved: for thou art my praise.

Jeremiah 17:14

I never thought a phone call would change the rest of my life. "We need you to come into the office and get set up with our breast surgeon. It's breast cancer."

THE UNEXPECTED NEWS

Days before, I noticed that my left breast was noticeably bigger than the right breast. I was in no pain whatsoever, so I didn't think too much of it, although it stayed in the back of my mind that I should check to see if it got bigger. Then one afternoon shortly after, while doing Zumba, my arm brushed up against my breast and I felt a knot. I went to the bathroom, took off my bra and began feeling around. Sure enough, there was something there. I began to feel on my right breast and I felt nothing. Back and forth I began feeling around on both breasts, and I knew something wasn't right. Later on that night, I called my mom and told her what I felt. She said it was probably a cyst. She got them all the time and so did my grandmother and my aunt. "Just call your doctor in the morning and have him check it out," she said. After I hung up the phone, I went to sleep thinking that's what it was.

The next day, I made an appointment with my primary care physician, and was able to get in on the same day. He did an exam, confirmed that there was a lump there, and ordered me to have a mammogram. The next day at work, while asking around for OBGYN referrals, I asked my assistant principal where she went, and she referred me to the breast center at the hospital in Annapolis. I made the appointment. I was nervous as I waited to be called into examination. I kept telling myself, "It's just a cyst."

Once in the room, the doctor examined my breast and wanted to schedule a biopsy of the lump the following day. That didn't sound good to me. In the back of my mind, having a biopsy meant there was something bigger going on. My mom told me that with a cyst they would just drain the fluid out and I'd be ok. I was plagued with questions. I kept thinking, what if it is cancer? What was I going to do? Did I catch it in time? Would I die? When I got home, I called my mom and she tried to assure me that it was just precautionary, that the lump would be benign and just have to be removed. My mom was in South Carolina and I lived in Maryland. I didn't want to go have the biopsy alone, so I called my aunt Vivian to come with me. The next day, my aunt Vivian and my uncle Anthony drove from Pennsylvania to accompany me to my appointment. As we were waiting in the lobby of the doctor's office, I wasn't as scared because Aunt Viv was with me and we were talking and laughing, distracting me from fearing the worst. The nurse called me back and the procedure began.

The doctor first did an ultrasound to locate the lump and numb the area where he would perform the biopsy. During the exam, I asked him if it was a cyst, and he immediately said no. "It's too hard to be a cyst. It's more than likely cancer," he said. I responded, "I refuse to believe it. It's not cancer. It's not cancer." I lie there praying in my mind that it was just a lump. He performed the biopsy and told me that they would call me when the results came, and he left the room. I got dressed and left the doctor's office with my aunt and uncle. I remember feeling somewhat scared. I was sore from the procedure, so I decided to take the following day off from work. That was on February 26, 2014.

The next day I laid around at home. I did some housework and caught up on some shows I'd missed. I was trying to keep busy and keep my mind at ease. It was going a mile a minute. I was anxiously anticipating the phone call from the doctor and dreading it at the same time. I knew I needed to hear the results of my biopsy, but I was scared they would say it was cancer. That was the longest 24 hours of my life. I started picking out the outfits I would take home for the weekend. I was getting excited about going to my first CIAA tournament with my best friends in Charlotte. I was ready for some fun. Around 1:35 pm, the phone rang and it was the nurse from the doctor's office. "Hello Miss Bouler," she said. "This is the nurse from the Breast Center. We need you to come in and make an appointment with the breast surgeon." I dropped to the floor. "Is it breast cancer?" I asked. She said it was, and I began to hyperventilate. She began asking questions about my medical insurance, but all I kept saying was, "I gotta call my momma." Tears were running down my face and I felt my chest tighten. When she realized I was in no position to answer any questions, she got off the phone.

Sitting on the side of my bed I let out a scream I didn't know I had in me. Hands shaking, I called my mother at work, crying, and I told her that the doctor called and that I had breast cancer. She screamed, "Oh Lord, I'm on my way, I'm on my way." I could hear her coworkers in the background saying they needed to call my stepfather to pick my mother up from work because she was so upset.

I called my best friends and told them the news. They were like my sisters and I knew I was going to need them now more than ever before. I needed their love and support. Crying, I kept asking them what I was going to do. My best friend Rinice said to me, "Tesha, we're gonna fight. That's what we're gonna do. We're gonna beat this." I appreciated the words of comfort, but it wasn't sinking in. All I could think about was whether or not I was going to die. At thirty-six years old, single, with no kids, how could I have breast cancer? There were so many things I had yet to accomplish. I had places to explore, people to see, babies to have. How could I have something that could potentially kill me? I called my aunts, Teresa and Vivian, to tell them the news, and it was my Aunt Vivian's voice that somehow brought me the peace that I needed. When I shared the news with her, crying and upset, she said in her calmest voice, "Tesha, just calm down." The more she said it, the calmer I became. It was as if God had suddenly sent a calmness over me, and the panic disappeared. When I got off the phone with Aunt Vivian, I went into my closet, closed the door, and had a talk with God.

I spoke to Him, saying, "God, it's me and you right now. I have breast cancer and I don't want it. You know I want a husband and a family. I'm ready to fight and beat this. Please help me." When I opened the door and walked out of the closet, it was like God had replaced the fear that had taken over my mind and body, and gave me strength and determination to face the beast head-on. I was ready to begin this journey.

THE LOVE AND COMFORT OF MOMMA

Momma flew to Maryland from South Carolina within a few days of getting the news. She stayed for about a week. During that time I made appointments to visit with the breast surgeon and the oncologist. I was feeling so many things as we drove to those appointments, but I was glad that my mother was there with me. When we arrived at the breast center in Annapolis that Tuesday morning, a feeling of anxiousness came over me. I didn't know what to expect. I had so many questions to ask. We were greeted by my nurse navigator, who assured me she would be by my side the entire way. That made me feel a little better too. She gave me resources I could use to help me along the way, and told me of support groups to join. Then she told me something I wasn't expecting to hear. "You're going to be okay. You're young and healthy. It's not a death trap anymore. We caught it before it got worse."

Hearing that was music to my ears. I'd always had the notion that cancer meant death, and so many people were dying from the disease. I just knew I was next. But when I heard I was going to be okay, it was like God was saying to me, "I got you. Don't worry. I'll take care of you and heal you." The nurse navigator grabbed my hand and hugged me, and I could feel some of the stress being lifted. I hung on to every word she said. Soon after, the breast surgeon came in, examined me, and explained to my mom and me the type of breast cancer I had. It was overwhelming hearing him talk about it. I couldn't believe that I actually had cancer. The more he talked, the more reality set in. Fear was rearing its ugly head again, even though I was told I was going to be okay. "Treatment needs to begin right away," he stated, "and that will be chemotherapy, a lumpectomy, and radiation." He asked if I had any children or was planning to have any kids in the near future. I told him I wanted to have kids someday, and he suggested I go and see a fertility specialist about having my eggs frozen before starting chemo. An appointment was made for that afternoon to discuss my options. It had never crossed my mind that the disease would impact my ability to have children. I knew I had to do whatever it took to secure my chances. The nurses and the fertility specialist were very thorough with answering all my questions, and the questions that my mother had as well. It was an easy decision for me to have the procedure done. The process would take three weeks, and it had to be completed rain, sleet, hail, or snow. I was ready.

The following day, I met with my oncologist. He was compassionate, knowledgeable, and understanding. He explained, to the letter, what my treatment would be, and assured me that I was going to be ok. I knew God had placed this doctor in my life to heal me. He not only won me over, but he won my mother over too. God was sending me signs from the very beginning that He was going to take care of me. All I had to do was trust and believe in Him.

After three weeks of completing my egg retrieval with the fertility specialist, I was ready to begin chemo. I had heard stories of how the treatment made cancer patients sick and weak. I'd heard the horror stories of how it made your hair fall out, and I was scared beyond measure. I didn't know what to expect. But love and support poured in from my family, friends, sorority sisters, and colleagues. It was like I had an army behind me. It gave me comfort that I was not alone.

NOTHING LIKE FAMILY

On the first day of treatment, my family drove from South Carolina to be with me. As my vitals were taken before treatment, tears were streaming down my face. I was so scared. I didn't know what to think. I was just ready to go home. I didn't want to be there. I'd seen people on television going through cancer treatment, and it made them sick and fatigued; their hair fell out; it looked like death. I was about to go through the same thing, and I was scared that those effects would happen to me. But my mother was right by my side. The nurse gave me a big hug and assured me that I would be alright. Once I was situated in my room, another nurse came in covered in scrubs from head to toe. She looked like someone from a scene in a science- fiction movie. Looking at her made me more nervous than ever. I tried to play it cool, but my nervousness showed on my face. When I asked her why she was dressed like that, she explained to me that she had to take the necessary precautions when administering my treatment. I could see the pharmacy from my room, where she went to get my medicine. The sign "Hazardous Materials" was on the door, and the other nurses were completely covered with scrubs and masks. I was terrified and ready to get it over with.

The nurse came back to the room with my first dose of medicine. It was bright red. Adriamycin or "The Red Devil," is what they called it. At that moment I couldn't believe that this "poison" was actually going to be put into my body. My eyes became fixated on the nurse as she transferred the medicine from the bag into a syringe. I was shaking and the tears were streaming again. My mom grabbed my hand and said to me, "Tesha, don't think of it as the Red Devil going inside you. That's Jesus' blood going inside you to heal you. It's Jesus' blood." As the medicine was going inside of my body, a calming spirit come over me. God was healing me right at that very moment. I knew I had a long journey ahead, but I knew I was going to make it. My faith had been renewed and I was determined to fight.

Chemo treatments lasted for four months. My hair began to fall out shortly after my third treatment. I completely lost it. Thoughts of what people would think of me flooded my mind. My uncle Anthony shaved my head because I couldn't bare seeing my hair fall out in clumps. Looking at myself completely bald, I felt like a different person. I wore scarves for a while, to cover my head. I even had a wig made to wear, but it wasn't me. I began to embrace my baldness and my inner beauty. Others began to see the beauty in me too. I was more confident in myself, and it made me a lot stronger. On my last day of chemo, I was ready and excited. The moment I had been waiting for had arrived. When a cancer patient completes their last chemo treatment, they get to ring the bell hanging in the waiting area of the infusion center, signifying a great accomplishment. My family and friends crowded the center. It was time for me to ring the bell. I was filled with so much emotion. The sound of that bell was the most beautiful sound I had ever heard. There was not a dry eye in the room. God got me through! Shortly after chemo, I underwent a six hour surgery to remove the tumor from my breast. It was the home stretch. There was but one more hurdle to jump— radiation. I was ready. I endured the hard part without experiencing any severe side effects. I never got sick while undergoing chemo. I was still able to go to work and live a somewhat normal life. I couldn't have gone through that part of my journey without the help of my family, friends, and my school family. They rallied together and gave me the strength I needed when I felt weak, and the encouragement to keep pushing forward. Radiation was daily for three months. My body began to feel the wear and tear of the treatment. I felt tired and worn out, but I knew God didn't bring me that far to leave me. Three days before my birthday in November, I completed my last radiation treatment. What a wonderful birthday gift God gave me. I did it. I beat it. I'm still alive, and I beat breast cancer!

BOLD REFLECTIONS

Whenever you are faced with a life-altering situation, know that it is okay to feel scared. It is okay to feel the emotions you are feeling, but don't let those emotions consume you. Be determined. And when life throws you a curveball, know that God will never leave you, and will always be by your side. All you have to do is trust and believe in Him and He will always take care of you. Surround yourself with loved ones that will support you, and have the mindset that you will overcome and come out on top!

About the Authors

Minister Eddie J. Bailey-Holden graduated from Shaw University, in Raleigh, NC, in 1993, with a Bachelor of Arts degree in Criminal Justice and Business Management. She then matriculated into Justice Fellowship International College in 2011, earning a Master's Degree in Biblical Counseling, and a Master of Arts in Ministry, in 2013. Eddie enjoyed 32 years of service with one of the world's most prestigious shipping companies, retiring in 2016.

Eddie, a faithful and dedicated woman of God, knew early on that God had a plan for her life. In 2012, she was called into the preaching ministry, and was ordained in 2016. She is the daughter of the late Bishops Eddie Jr. and Geraldine Newton Bailey. Eddie has been married for 26 years to William "Bill" Holden. Together, they have four sons and seven grandchildren.

For more information,
contact Eddie Bailey-Holden at
ebholden@bellsouth.net.

About the Authors

Lenase Shands was born in Tarrytown, Georgia and raised in Cleveland, Ohio. She currently resides in Maryland with her husband of 26 years, Samuel T. Shands. Together they share 7 children, 14 grandchildren and 6 great-grandchildren. She retired from George Washington University Hospital after 25 years of service in 1994, and earned an Associate's Degree in Health Care from ACT College in 2007.

Lenase has been a member of Mount Calvary Baptist Church for 25 years, under the leadership of Pastor Charles. E. Cato, Sr. She serves on several ministries and is the VP of Education for Calvary Speaks Toastmaster Club. She has traveled to Kenya for missionary work and was recently licensed as a Minister. Her mission is to minister to all and share the gospel of Jesus.

For a more detailed information,
contact me Lenase Shands at
Shandslen48@outlook.com.

Michele Noel-Peake is co-owner of Peake Point Productions. She has over 20 years of leadership experience with Fortune 500 companies and has written many successful employee relations programs, including winning diversity strategies for Managers and Executive Leaders. She has been interviewed for both radio and print for her work as a Certified Life Coach and community advocate, speaking out against domestic violence, as well as for her work with youth in her community. She holds a Bachelor's of Science in Business Administration.

As a licensed Minister, Michele leads several ministries in her church. She is married to Rodney and they have two daughters, Zarina and Nia.

For more information,
contact Michele Noel-Peake at
mnoelpeake@gmail.com.

About the Authors

Felicia Evans Long is a native of Lumberton, North Carolina but resides in Rockville, Maryland. She received a Bachelor of Arts in Sociology from Shaw University in 1994, and a Master of Business Administration from the University of Phoenix in 2008. Felicia has been involved with many initiatives from the University and has been featured in their *Phoenix Focus* magazine for entrepreneurs. She is a member of Delta Sigma Theta Sorority, Inc., Lumberton Chamber of Commerce, and a volunteer for Fight for Children, Inc., in Washington, DC.

Felicia is the owner of Sweet Candy Café, a confectionery store in Lumberton, North Carolina. She is also the founder of Candy Kids Wear Blazers, an organization established in 2017 that teaches young girls about the many facets of confection, in addition to professionalism, entrepreneurship, and hospitality. Felicia is passionate about being a community servant, giving back and leading by example.

For more information,
contact Felicia Evans Long at
SweetCandyCafeNC@gmail.com,
or visit her website:
SweetCandyCafe.com.

Juanita Payne was born in Jamaica Queens, but currently resides in Waldorf, MD and is the mother of three amazing children, Jasmine, Isaiah, and Jade. Juanita earned a Bachelor's Degree in Computer Systems, a Master's in Internet Security, and a second Master's in Cyber Security.

Juanita is an IT Specialist for the National Oceanic and Atmospheric Administration (NOAA), and is also a member of The National Association of Professional Women (NAPW).

In the ceaseless pursuit of personal freedom, financial stability, and progressive thinking, Juanita plans to continue leading and influencing the world through her strong connection with God, while continuing to thrive in eternal love.

For more information,
contact Juanita Payne at
Chose2bchosn@gmail.com.

About the Authors

Sonya M. Hall-Brown is a wife, mother of five, and grandmother of three. She is dedicated to letting single parents know that their life is not ruined because they have children out of wedlock.

Sonya is was born in Bronx, NY, and relocated to Blackstock, SC. She received her degree from Columbia Junior College in Columbia, SC, which is now South University. Sonya is the Founder and CEO of L and S Cleaning, Express, LLC. She is an active member of St. Luke Baptist Church in Winnsboro, SC where she is a youth advisor and assistant financial secretary.

Contact Sonya M. Hall-Brown at
smbrown1226@live.com.

Tonya Mackey Harris is an inspired motivational speaker, business owner, mother of two, and Learning Leader for Children's Healthcare of Atlanta.

She has over 25 years of experience in training, consulting, leadership and organizational development, change management, and motivational speaking. Her niche is helping professionals shape their strategic direction, and encouraging leaders to achieve their goals.

Her goal, however, is to be an influencer through her testimony of surviving breast cancer and mental illness in her family. Her story is powerful, yet uplifting, in how she has taken her journey and shaped it into her motivation to help others. Her focus is to help others succeed at moving past barriers to find purpose.

She serves in multiple ministries within her church as a missionary, leadership development advisor and teacher. She has a Master's in Management and is certified in both Strategic Organizational Leadership and Executive Coaching.

Contact Tonya Mackey Harris at
latonayaaka@comcast.net.

About the Authors

Vatesha Bouler was born in Chester, South Carolina and currently resides in Laurel, Maryland. She received her Bachelor's Degree in Early Childhood Education from the University of South Carolina Aiken. Vatesha holds a Master's of Education in Divergent Learning from Columbia College in Columbia, South Carolina. She is a member of Alpha Kappa Alpha Sorority, Inc. and a charter member of the Patuxent River Chapter of Top Ladies of Distinction, Inc. She is a member of New Psalmist Baptist Church.

Vatesha is an educator of 17 years. She currently teaches kindergarten with the Prince George's County Public Schools in Maryland. She believes in living life to the fullest. She is a woman of faith and believes that God will always be by your side.

Contact Vatesha Bouler at
vateshab@aol.com.

Tammy Woodard was born in Chester, South Carolina, and currently resides in Fort Mill, SC. She received her Bachelor's in Computer Information Systems from Shaw University in 1992, and her Master's in Cyber Security from the University of Maryland in 2016. She is a Silver Star member of Alpha Kappa Alpha Sorority, Inc., and an active member of Mt. Calvary Baptist Church of Lanham, MD, where she served as the Director of Public Relations/Marketing for the Women's Ministry, and group leader for the AWANA Youth Ministry.

As a transformational speaker/life coach, Tammy is dedicated to helping others discover their gifts and reach their full potential. She is a bestselling author for her collaborative efforts in the book "Soul Talk," released in 2017, and Lead Ambassador of the "Cheryl Brand Ambassador Program" for Williamson Media Group, LLC and Cheryl Polote Williamson, LLC. She is also the owner of Woodard Worldwide Visions, LLC.

Tammy is the mother of two sons, Thomas Jr. (23) & Damahje (15), whom she loves dearly. She is a virtuous woman of God, who has the heart to help those in need and serve others. Her favorite scripture is Jeremiah 29:11(NIV), "For I know the plans I have for you, declares the LORD," "plans to prosper you and not to harm you, plans to give you hope and a future."

Sources

Unless otherwise indicated, scripture quotations are from the Holy Bible, King James Version. All rights reserved.

Scriptures marked ESV are taken from English Standard Version®. Copyright © 2001 by Crossway, a publishing ministry of Good News Publishers. All rights reserved.

Scriptures marked NASB are taken from the New American Standard Bible®. Copyright © 1960, 1962, 1963, 1968, 1971, 1972, 1973, 1975, 1977, 1995 by The Lockman Foundation. Used by permission.

Scriptures marked NIV are taken from the New International Version®. Copyright © 1973, 1978, 1984, 2011 by Biblica, Inc.™. All rights reserved.

Scriptures marked NKJV are taken from the New King James Version ®. Copyright © 1982 by Thomas Nelson. All rights reserved.

Scriptures marked NLT are taken from the New Living Translation®. Copyright © 1996, 2004, 2007, 2013 by Tyndale House Foundation. All rights reserved.

To Book for Coaching & Speaking Events:

Contact Tammy Woodard
@ 443-292-2252 or
Designedpurposely@yahoo.com

On Facebook @ Tammy Woodard &
Instagram @ TammyTeaches

Also available for Private Book Signings,
Church Events and Conferences.

CREATING DISTINCTIVE BOOKS WITH INTENTIONAL RESULTS

We're a collaborative group of creative masterminds with a mission to produce high-quality books to position you for monumental success in the marketplace.

Our professional team of writers, editors, designers, and marketing strategists work closely together to ensure that every detail of your book is a clear representation of the message in your writing.

Want to know more?
Write to us at info@publishyourgift.com
or call (888) 949-6228

Discover great books, exclusive offers, and more at
www.PublishYourGift.com

Connect with us on social media

@publishyourgift